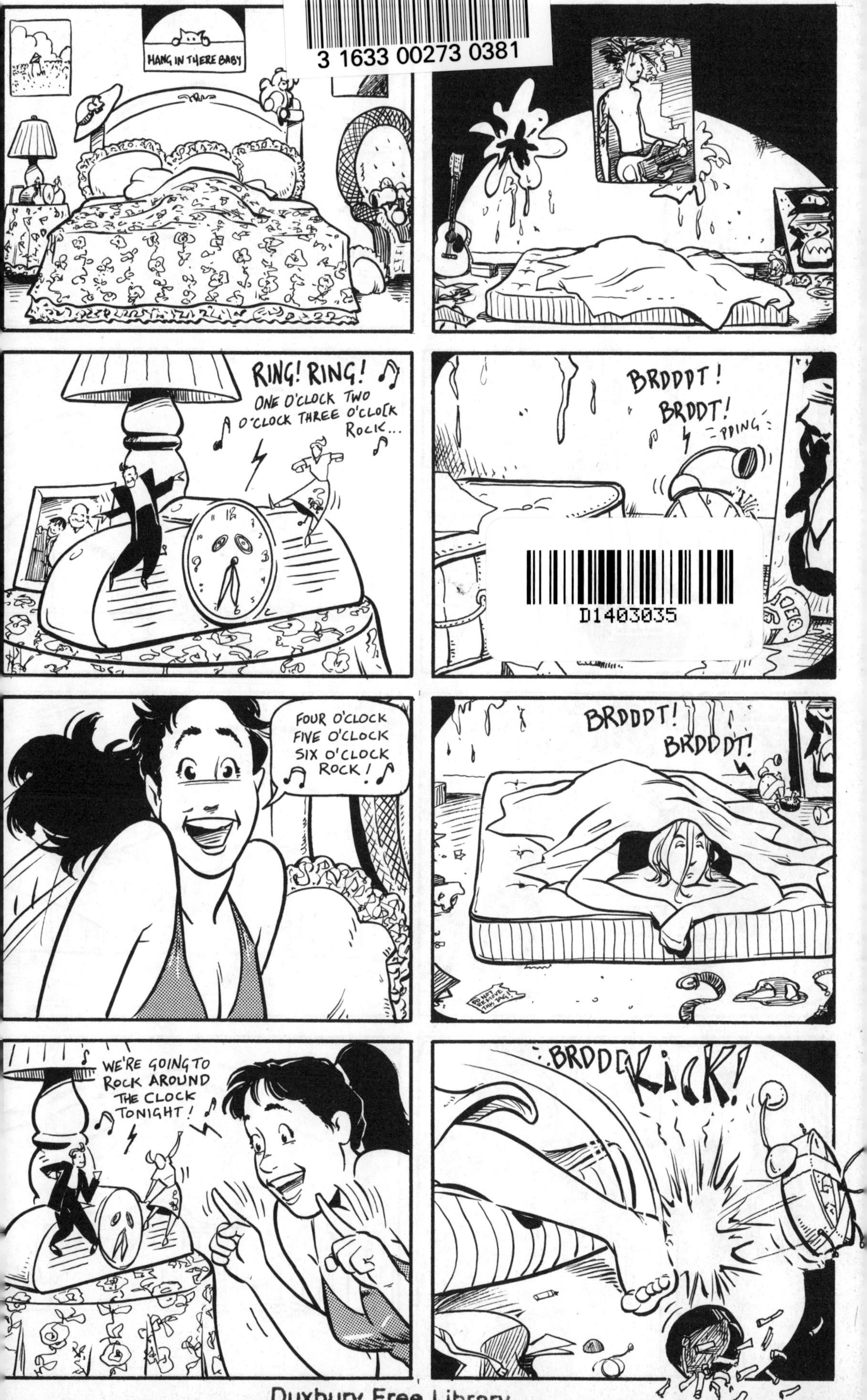
HANG IN THERE BABY
RING! RING!
ONE O'CLOCK TWO O'CLOCK THREE O'CLOCK ROCK...
BRDDDT! BRDDT!
PDING
FOUR O'CLOCK FIVE O'CLOCK SIX O'CLOCK ROCK!
BRDDDT! BRDDDT!
DO NOT REMOVE THIS TAG!
WE'RE GOING TO ROCK AROUND THE CLOCK TONIGHT!
BRDDD KICK!

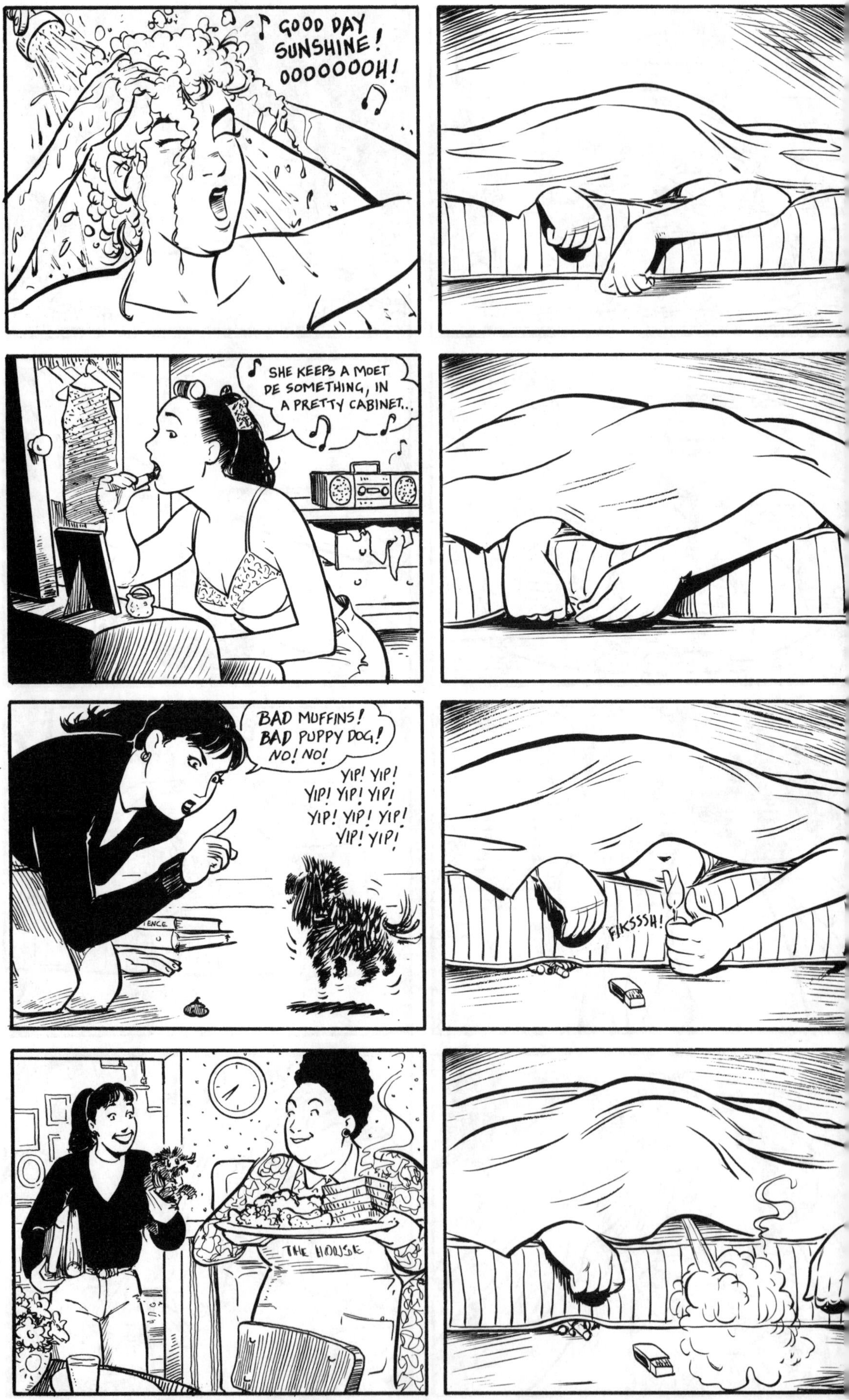
GOOD DAY SUNSHINE! OOOOOOOH!
SHE KEEPS A MOET DE SOMETHING, IN A PRETTY CABINET...
BAD MUFFINS! BAD PUPPY DOG! NO! NO!
YIP! YIP! YIP! YIP! YIP! YIP! YIP! YIP! YIP! YIP!
FIKSSSH!
THE HOUSE

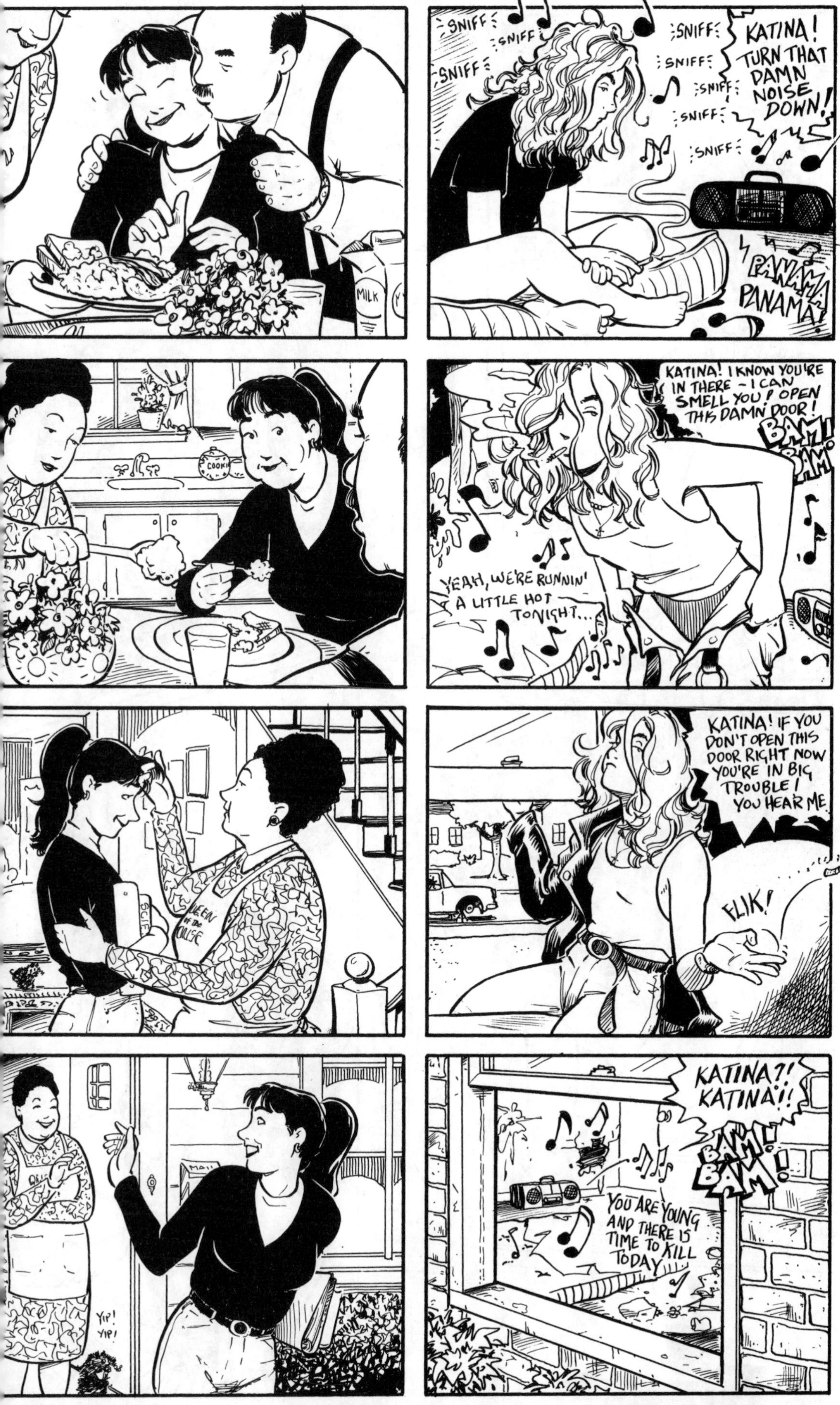

SNIFF SNIFF SNIFF SNIFF SNIFF SNIFF SNIFF SNIFF
KATINA! TURN THAT DAMN NOISE DOWN!
PANAMA PANAMA!
KATINA! I KNOW YOU'RE IN THERE - I CAN SMELL YOU! OPEN THIS DAMN DOOR!
BAM! BAM!
YEAH, WE'RE RUNNIN' A LITTLE HOT TONIGHT...
QUEEN of the HOUSE
KATINA! IF YOU DON'T OPEN THIS DOOR RIGHT NOW YOU'RE IN BIG TROUBLE! YOU HEAR ME
FLIK!
KATINA?! KATINA!!
BAM! BAM!
YOU ARE YOUNG AND THERE IS TIME TO KILL TODAY
YIP! YIP!

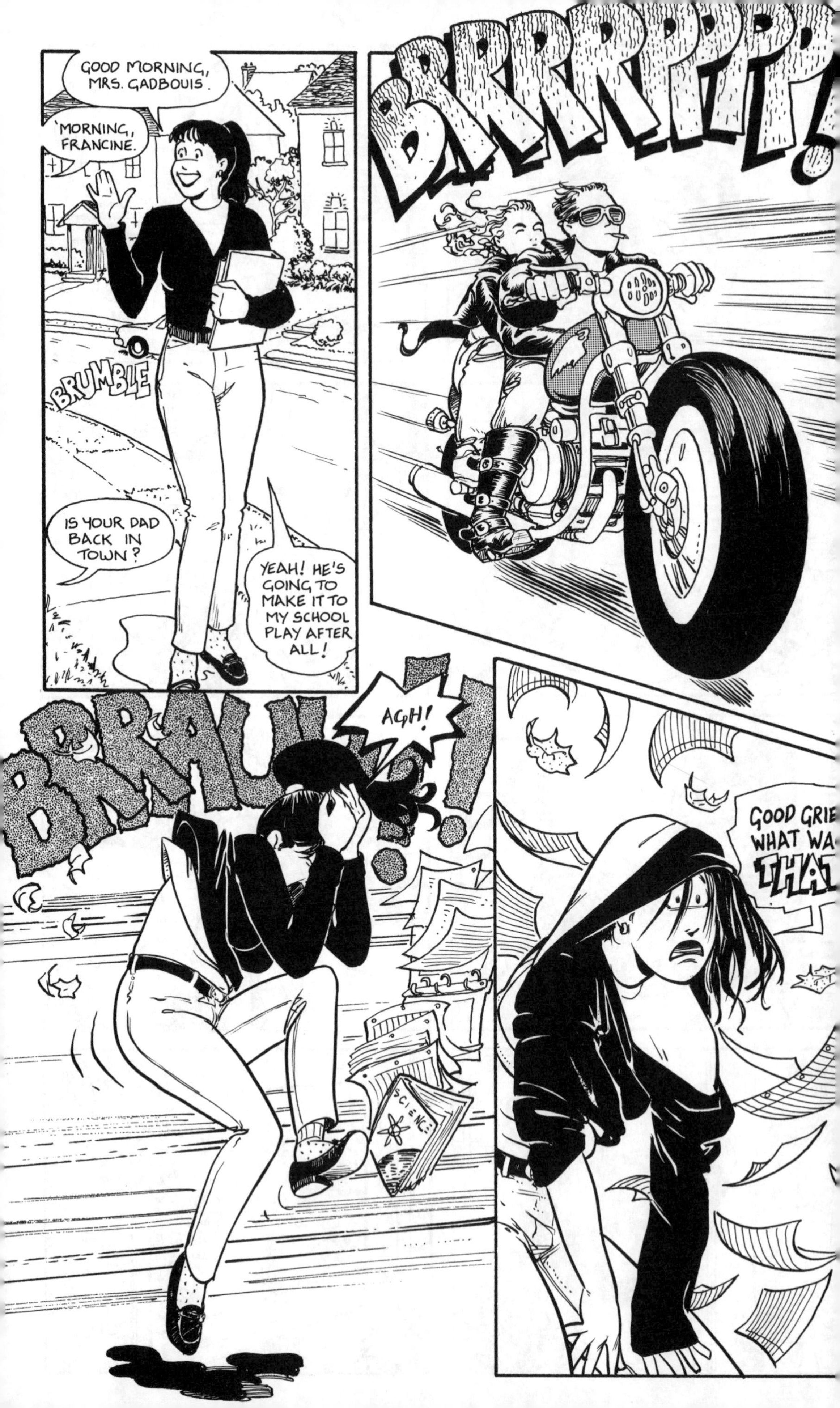
GOOD MORNING, MRS. GADBOUIS.
'MORNING, FRANCINE.
BRUMBLE
IS YOUR DAD BACK IN TOWN?
YEAH! HE'S GOING TO MAKE IT TO MY SCHOOL PLAY AFTER ALL!
BRRRRPPPP!
AGH!
GOOD GRIE
WHAT WA
THAT

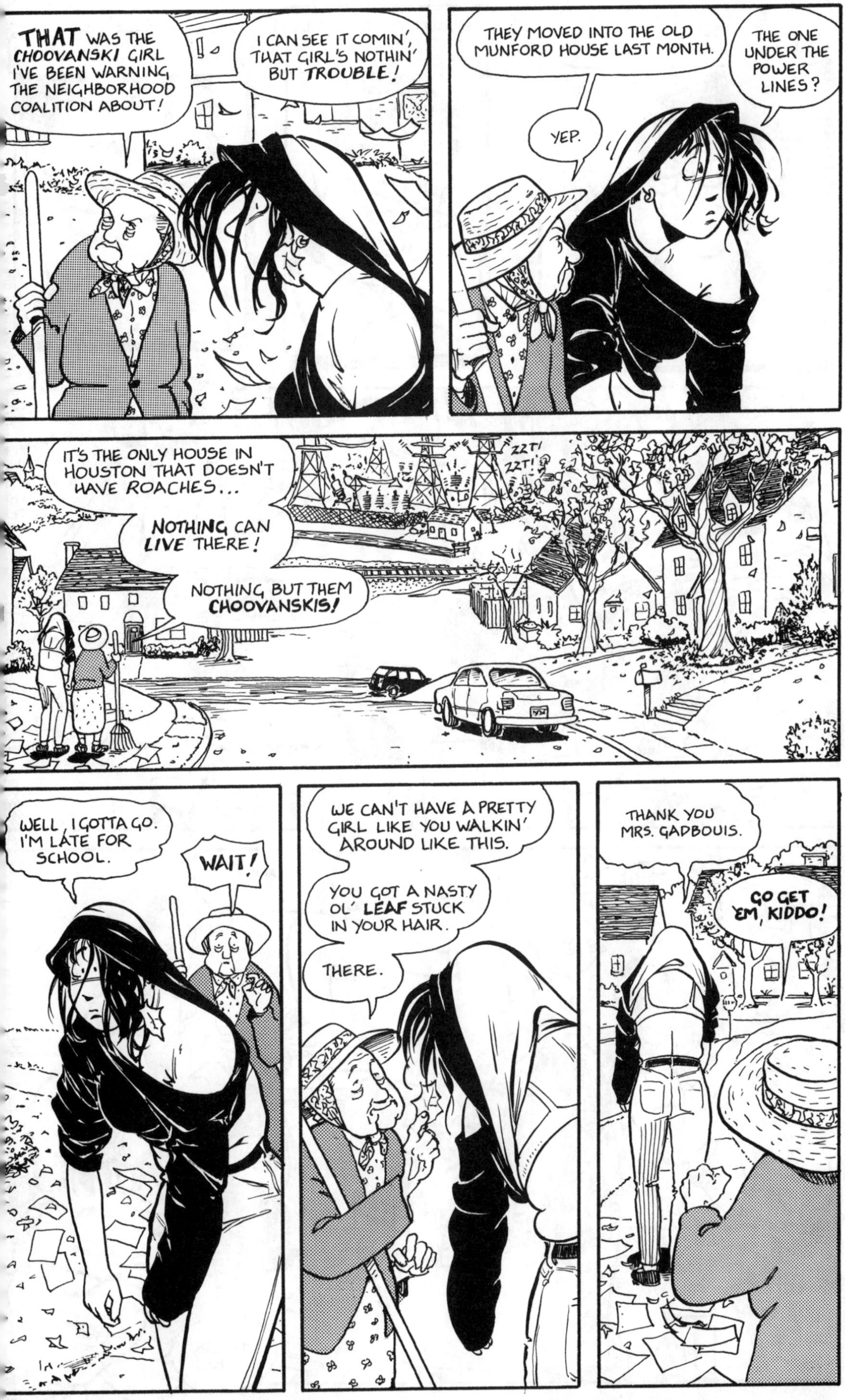
THAT WAS THE CHOOVANSKI GIRL I'VE BEEN WARNING THE NEIGHBORHOOD COALITION ABOUT!
I CAN SEE IT COMIN', THAT GIRL'S NOTHIN' BUT TROUBLE!
THEY MOVED INTO THE OLD MUNFORD HOUSE LAST MONTH.
THE ONE UNDER THE POWER LINES?
YEP.
IT'S THE ONLY HOUSE IN HOUSTON THAT DOESN'T HAVE ROACHES...
NOTHING CAN LIVE THERE!
NOTHING BUT THEM CHOOVANSKIS!
ZZT! ZZT!
WELL, I GOTTA GO. I'M LATE FOR SCHOOL.
WAIT!
WE CAN'T HAVE A PRETTY GIRL LIKE YOU WALKIN' AROUND LIKE THIS.
YOU GOT A NASTY OL' LEAF STUCK IN YOUR HAIR.
THERE.
THANK YOU MRS. GADBOUIS.
GO GET 'EM, KIDDO!

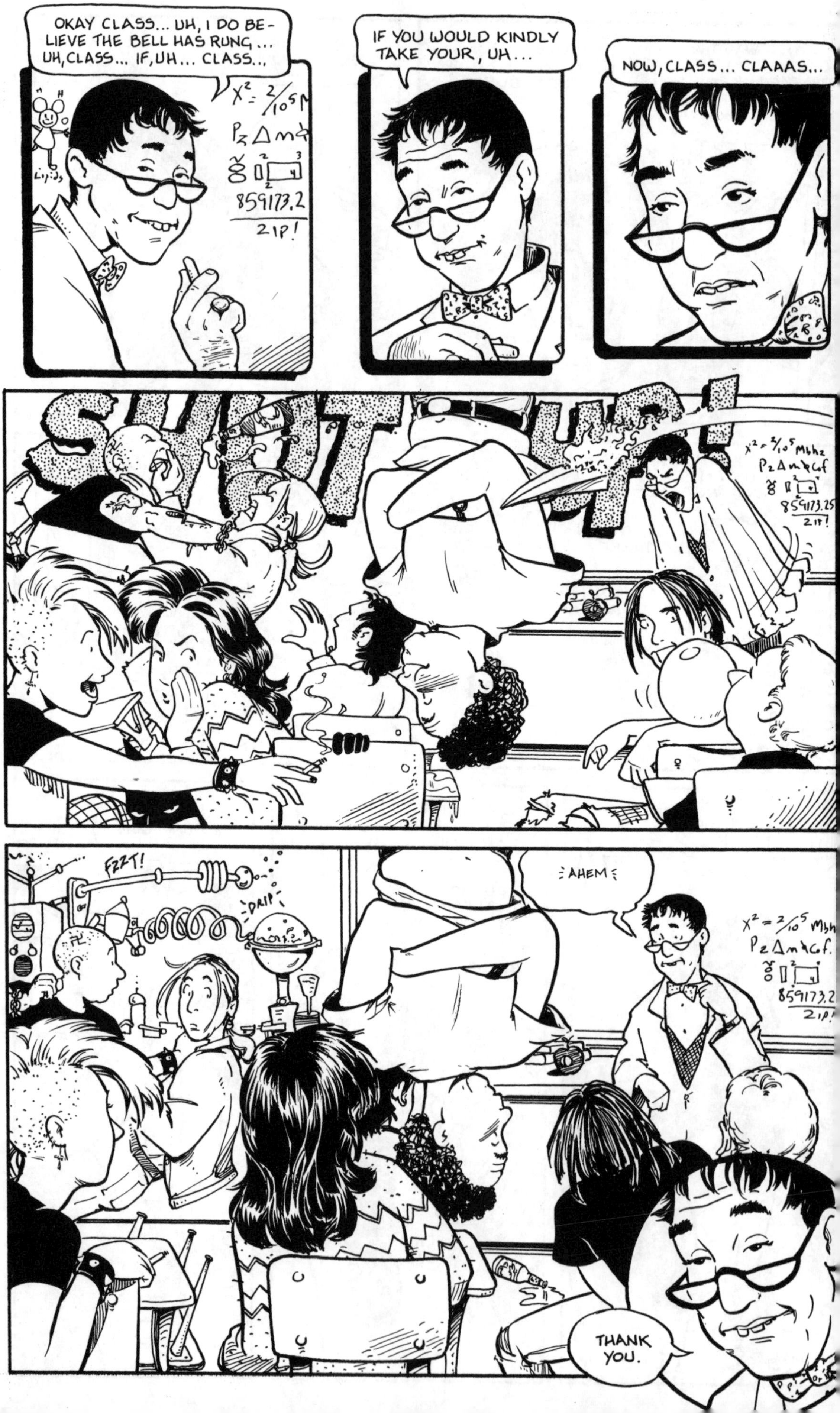

OKAY CLASS... UH, I DO BE-LIEVE THE BELL HAS RUNG... UH, CLASS... IF, UH... CLASS...
IF YOU WOULD KINDLY TAKE YOUR, UH...
NOW, CLASS... CLAAAS...
FZZT!
DRIP
AHEM
THANK YOU.

NOW THEN, IF YOU WILL RECALL, LAST WEEK WE WERE DISCUSSING THE **NICOLAIDE'S** THEORY OF CHAOS AS IT APPLIES TO THE THERMONUCLEAR LAWS OF DYNAMICS.

LAWS OF DYNAMICS.

OR, FOR THOSE OF YOU DESIRING A MORE PEDESTRIAN TERM...

220B

HEY! BETTIE!

...TIME TRAVEL!

FORGET IT, DAVE.

...EXPRESSIONS OF THE HEART IN A FEW LINES...

...THAT THE NOVELIST MIGHT TAKE PAGES TO DESCRIBE.

221B

SO... WHO WANTS TO GO FIRST?

COME ON NOW. I GAVE YOU GUYS ALL WEEKEND TO WRITE A POEM.

FREDDIE, HOW ABOUT YOU?

I THINK THAT A POEM AS A A TREE WHO SLINKY LOVE — EDGAR

THURS POET

≈AHEM≈ The Breast by Frederick Femur

HA! HA! HA! HÄ! HÄ!

ALRIGHT CLASS, LET'S GIVE MR. FEMUR HIS CONSTITUTIONAL RIGHT. BESIDES, I'D LIKE TO HEAR WHAT HE HAS TO SAY ON THE SUBJECT.

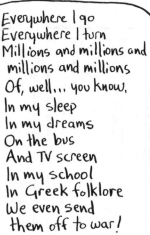

Everywhere I go
Everywhere I turn
Millions and millions and
  millions and millions
Of, well... you know.
In my sleep
In my dreams
On the bus
And TV screen
In my school
In Greek folklore
We even send
  them off to war!

Politicians
New rock stars
Is there no end
to where they are?

But I'm not sad
In fact, I'm glad!
What am I, stupid?

Don't answer that.

I'm glad they're here
What can I say
If not for them,
I might be GAY!

Not that there's anything wrong with that. The end.

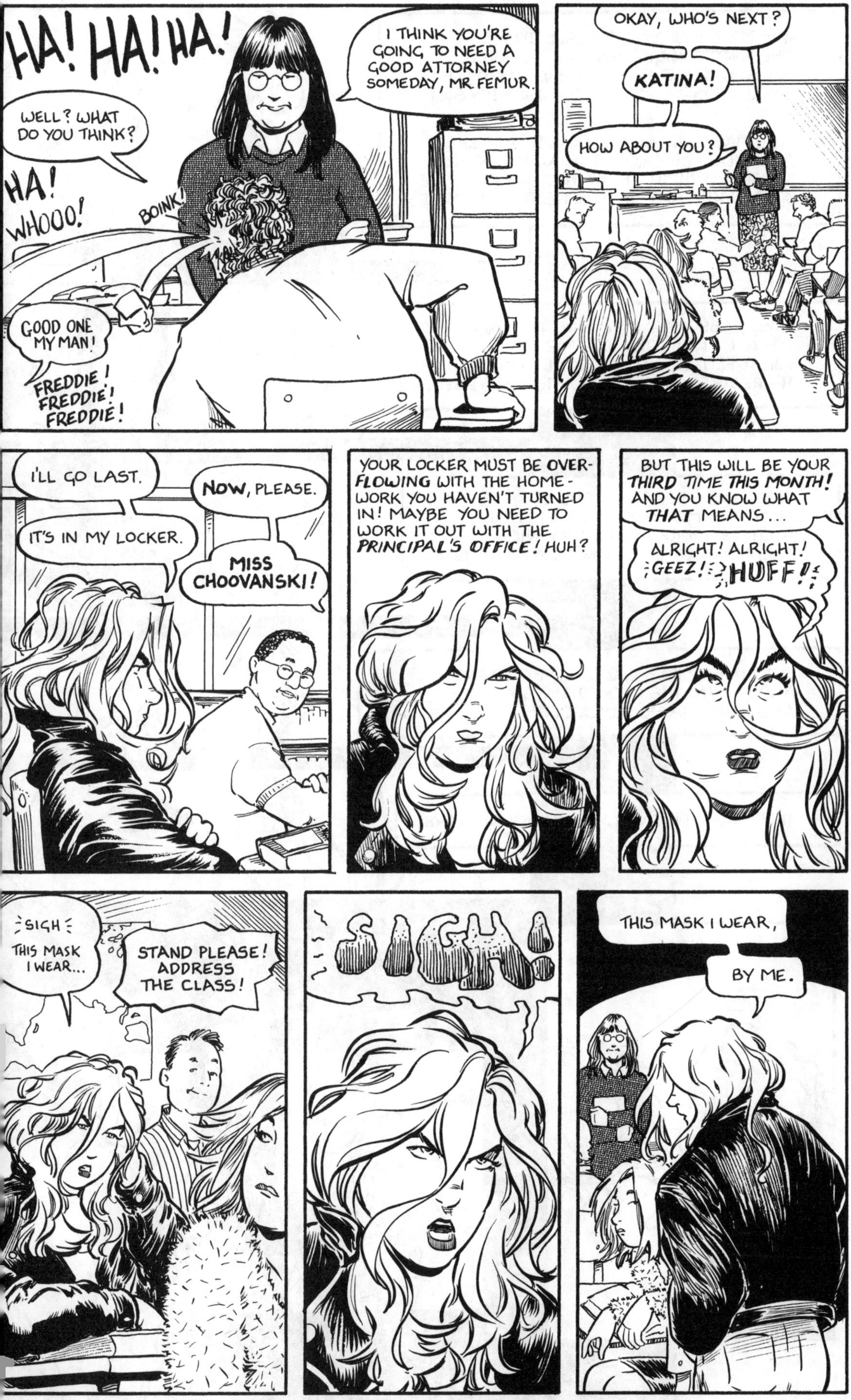
HA! HA! HA!
WELL? WHAT DO YOU THINK?
HA!
WHOOO!
BOINK!
GOOD ONE MY MAN!
FREDDIE! FREDDIE! FREDDIE!
I THINK YOU'RE GOING TO NEED A GOOD ATTORNEY SOMEDAY, MR. FEMUR.
OKAY, WHO'S NEXT?
KATINA!
HOW ABOUT YOU?
I'LL GO LAST.
IT'S IN MY LOCKER.
NOW, PLEASE.
MISS CHOOVANSKI!
YOUR LOCKER MUST BE OVER-FLOWING WITH THE HOME-WORK YOU HAVEN'T TURNED IN! MAYBE YOU NEED TO WORK IT OUT WITH THE PRINCIPAL'S OFFICE! HUH?
BUT THIS WILL BE YOUR THIRD TIME THIS MONTH! AND YOU KNOW WHAT THAT MEANS...
ALRIGHT! ALRIGHT! GEEZ! HUFF!
SIGH
THIS MASK I WEAR...
STAND PLEASE! ADDRESS THE CLASS!
SIGH!
THIS MASK I WEAR,
BY ME.

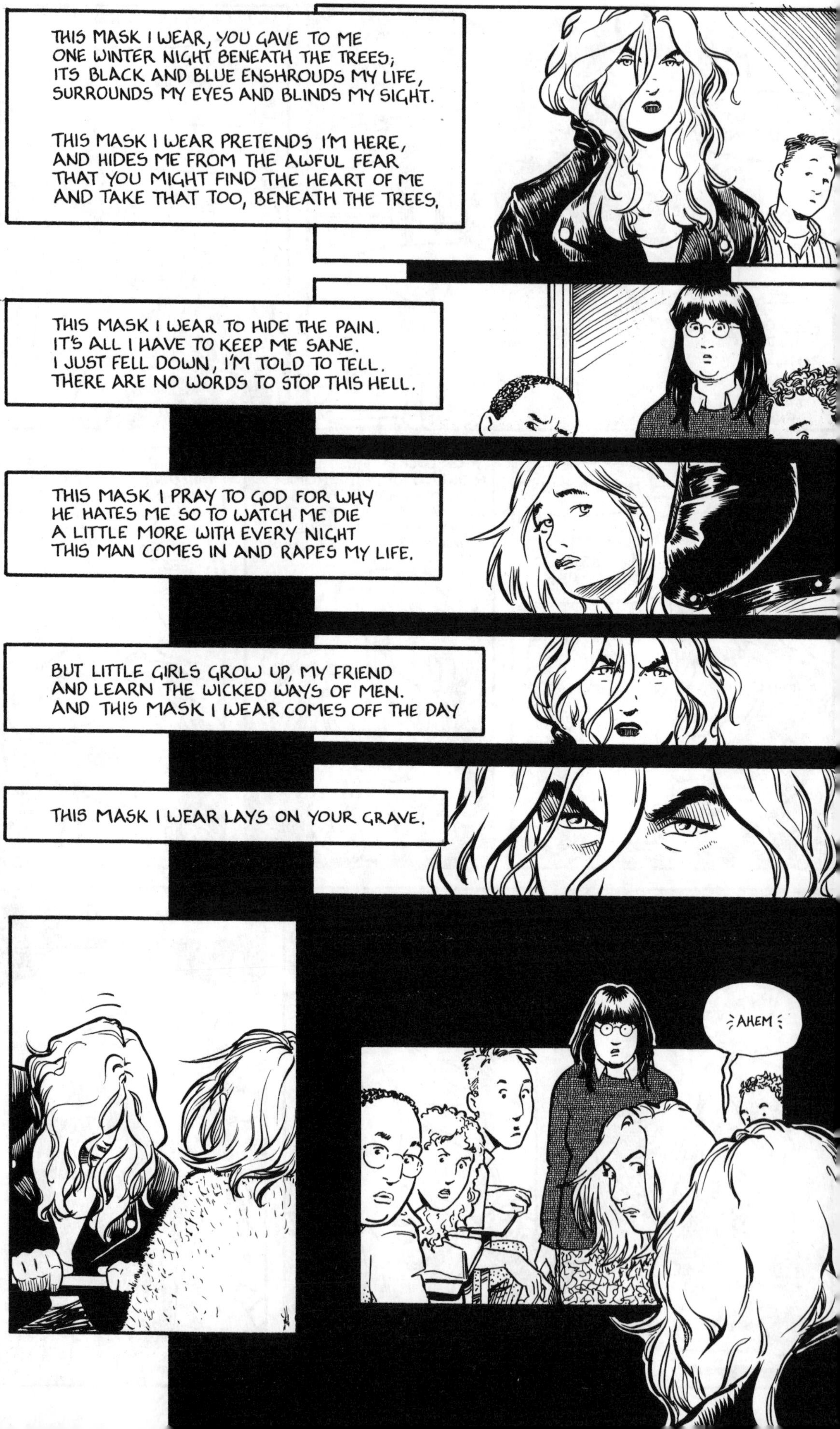
THIS MASK I WEAR, YOU GAVE TO ME
ONE WINTER NIGHT BENEATH THE TREES;
ITS BLACK AND BLUE ENSHROUDS MY LIFE,
SURROUNDS MY EYES AND BLINDS MY SIGHT.
THIS MASK I WEAR PRETENDS I'M HERE,
AND HIDES ME FROM THE AWFUL FEAR
THAT YOU MIGHT FIND THE HEART OF ME
AND TAKE THAT TOO, BENEATH THE TREES.
THIS MASK I WEAR TO HIDE THE PAIN.
IT'S ALL I HAVE TO KEEP ME SANE.
I JUST FELL DOWN, I'M TOLD TO TELL.
THERE ARE NO WORDS TO STOP THIS HELL.
THIS MASK I PRAY TO GOD FOR WHY
HE HATES ME SO TO WATCH ME DIE
A LITTLE MORE WITH EVERY NIGHT
THIS MAN COMES IN AND RAPES MY LIFE.
BUT LITTLE GIRLS GROW UP, MY FRIEND
AND LEARN THE WICKED WAYS OF MEN.
AND THIS MASK I WEAR COMES OFF THE DAY
THIS MASK I WEAR LAYS ON YOUR GRAVE.
AHEM

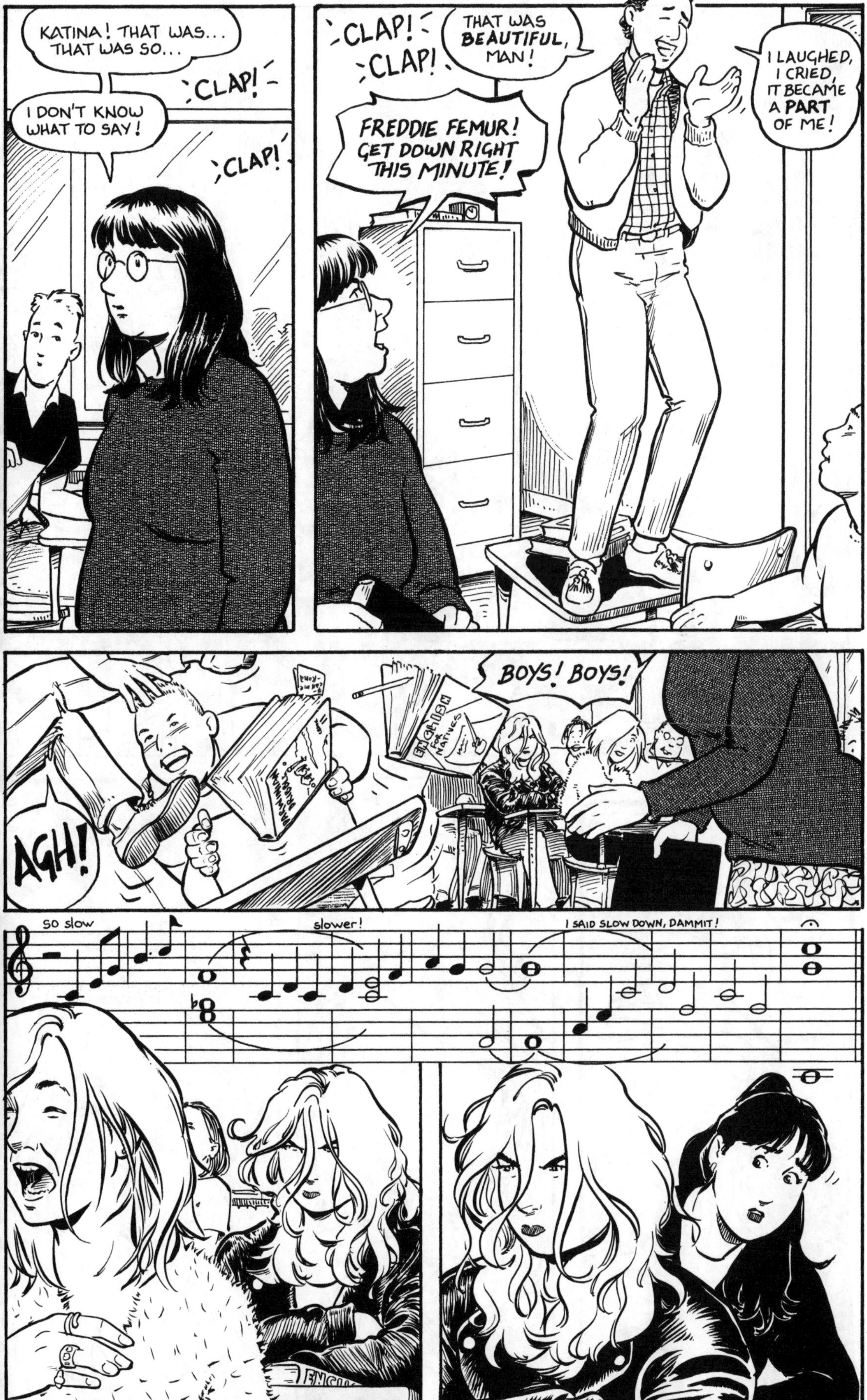
KATINA! THAT WAS... THAT WAS SO...
CLAP!
I DON'T KNOW WHAT TO SAY!
CLAP!
CLAP!
CLAP!
THAT WAS BEAUTIFUL, MAN!
I LAUGHED, I CRIED, IT BECAME A PART OF ME!
FREDDIE FEMUR! GET DOWN RIGHT THIS MINUTE!
BOYS! BOYS!
AGH!
ENGLISH FOR NATIVES
so slow
slower!
I SAID SLOW DOWN, DAMMIT!

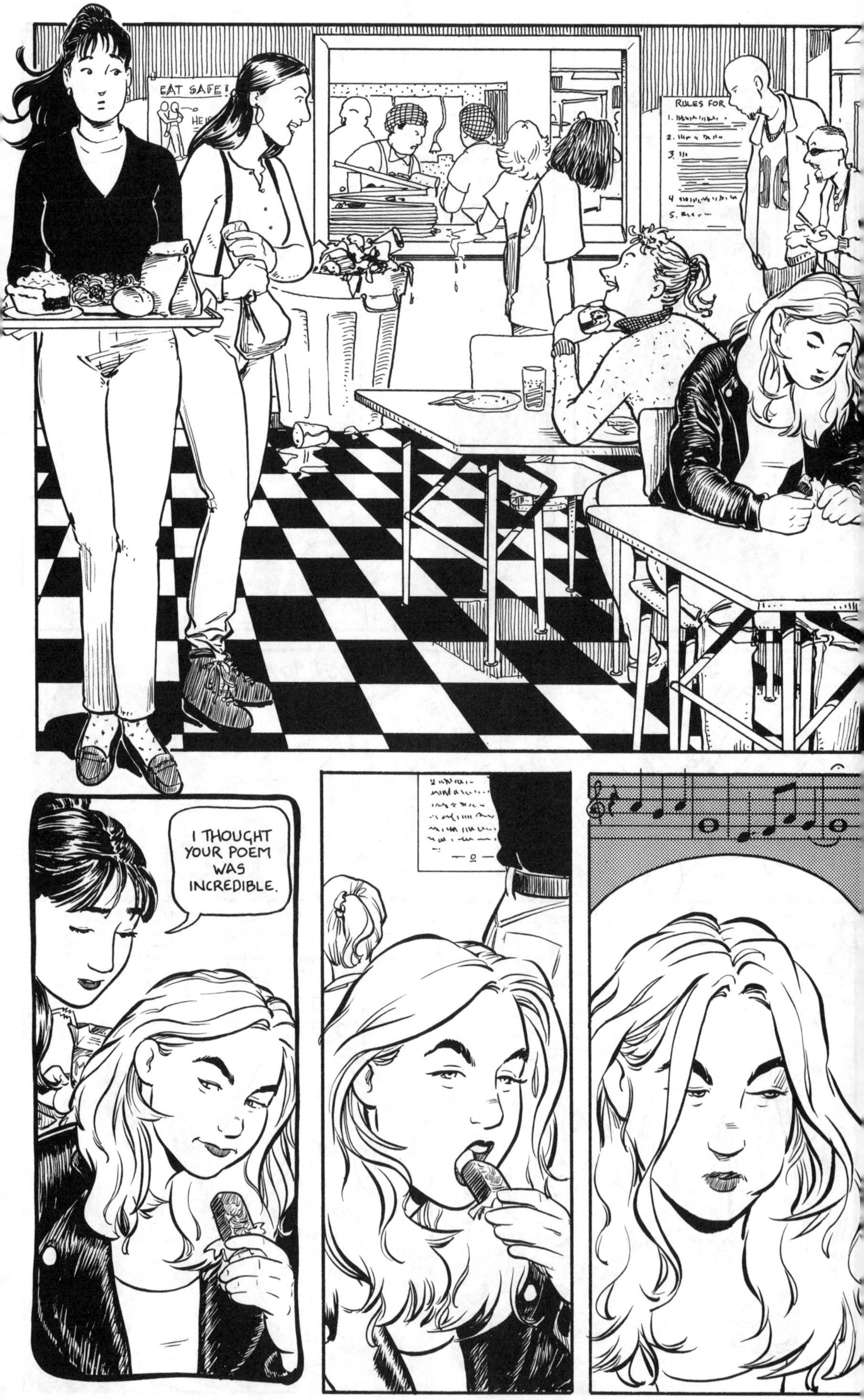
EAT SAFE!
RULES FOR
I THOUGHT YOUR POEM WAS INCREDIBLE.

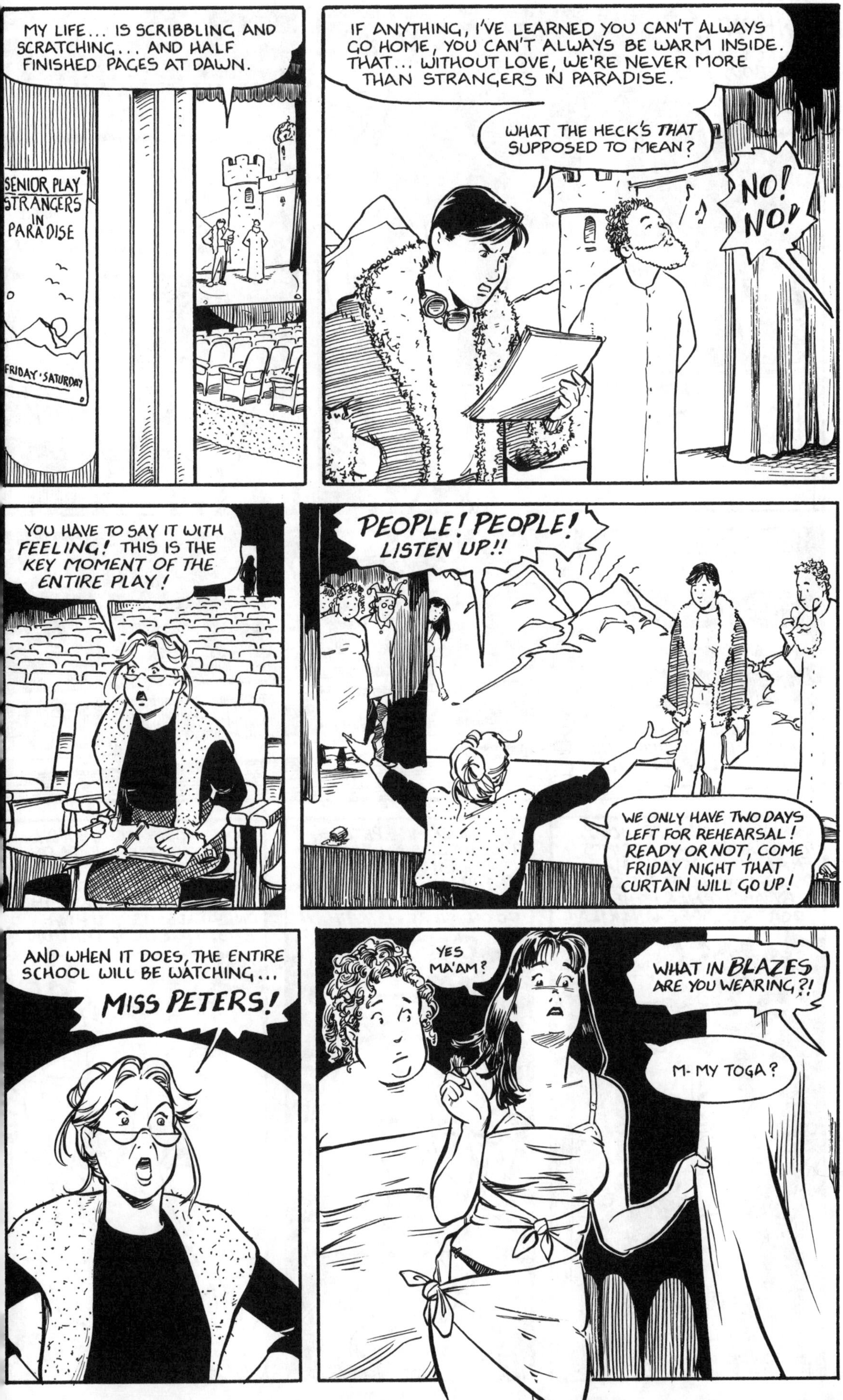

MY LIFE... IS SCRIBBLING AND SCRATCHING... AND HALF FINISHED PAGES AT DAWN.
SENIOR PLAY
STRANGERS IN PARADISE
FRIDAY · SATURDAY
IF ANYTHING, I'VE LEARNED YOU CAN'T ALWAYS GO HOME, YOU CAN'T ALWAYS BE WARM INSIDE. THAT... WITHOUT LOVE, WE'RE NEVER MORE THAN STRANGERS IN PARADISE.
WHAT THE HECK'S THAT SUPPOSED TO MEAN?
NO! NO!
YOU HAVE TO SAY IT WITH FEELING! THIS IS THE KEY MOMENT OF THE ENTIRE PLAY!
PEOPLE! PEOPLE! LISTEN UP!!
WE ONLY HAVE TWO DAYS LEFT FOR REHEARSAL! READY OR NOT, COME FRIDAY NIGHT THAT CURTAIN WILL GO UP!
AND WHEN IT DOES, THE ENTIRE SCHOOL WILL BE WATCHING... MISS PETERS!
YES MA'AM?
WHAT IN BLAZES ARE YOU WEARING?!
M- MY TOGA?

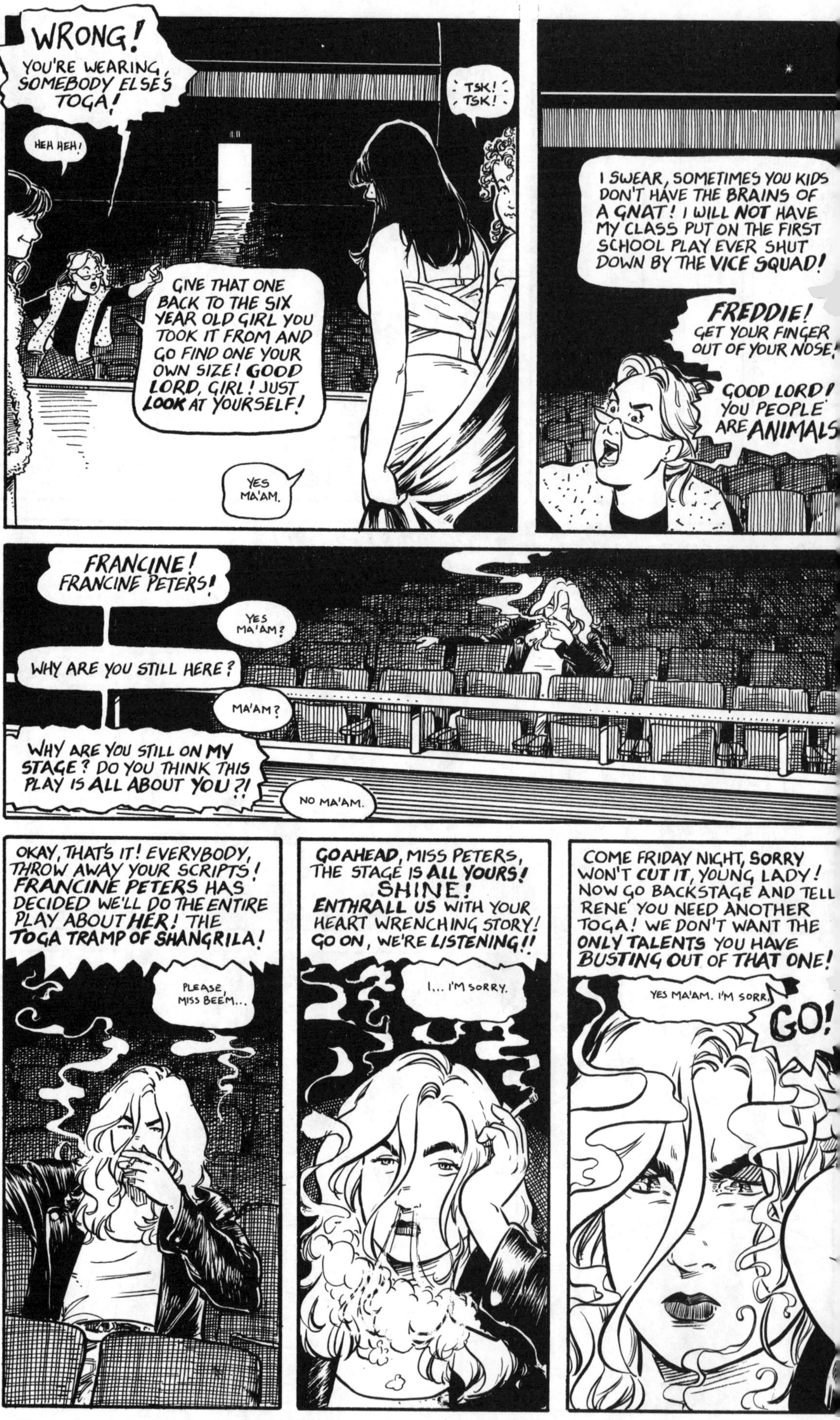
WRONG!
YOU'RE WEARING SOMEBODY ELSE'S TOGA!
HEH HEH!
TSK! TSK!
GIVE THAT ONE BACK TO THE SIX YEAR OLD GIRL YOU TOOK IT FROM AND GO FIND ONE YOUR OWN SIZE! GOOD LORD, GIRL! JUST LOOK AT YOURSELF!
YES MA'AM.
I SWEAR, SOMETIMES YOU KIDS DON'T HAVE THE BRAINS OF A GNAT! I WILL NOT HAVE MY CLASS PUT ON THE FIRST SCHOOL PLAY EVER SHUT DOWN BY THE VICE SQUAD!
FREDDIE! GET YOUR FINGER OUT OF YOUR NOSE!
GOOD LORD! YOU PEOPLE ARE ANIMALS
FRANCINE! FRANCINE PETERS!
YES MA'AM?
WHY ARE YOU STILL HERE?
MA'AM?
WHY ARE YOU STILL ON MY STAGE? DO YOU THINK THIS PLAY IS ALL ABOUT YOU?!
NO MA'AM.
OKAY, THAT'S IT! EVERYBODY, THROW AWAY YOUR SCRIPTS! FRANCINE PETERS HAS DECIDED WE'LL DO THE ENTIRE PLAY ABOUT HER! THE TOGA TRAMP OF SHANGRILA!
PLEASE, MISS BEEM...
GO AHEAD, MISS PETERS, THE STAGE IS ALL YOURS! SHINE! ENTHRALL US WITH YOUR HEART WRENCHING STORY! GO ON, WE'RE LISTENING!!
I... I'M SORRY.
COME FRIDAY NIGHT, SORRY WON'T CUT IT, YOUNG LADY! NOW GO BACKSTAGE AND TELL RENE YOU NEED ANOTHER TOGA! WE DON'T WANT THE ONLY TALENTS YOU HAVE BUSTING OUT OF THAT ONE!
YES MA'AM. I'M SORR
GO!

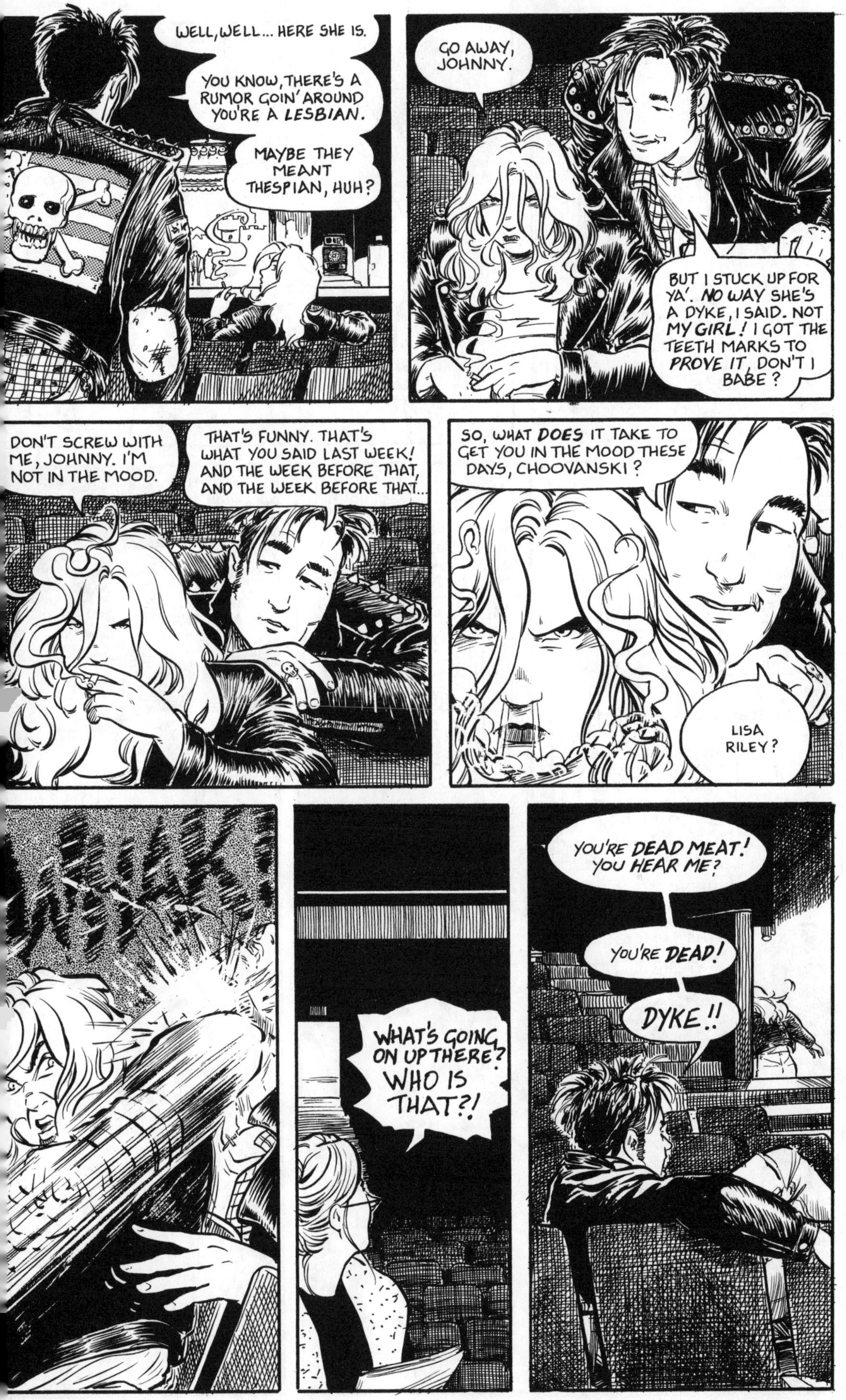
WELL, WELL... HERE SHE IS.
YOU KNOW, THERE'S A RUMOR GOIN' AROUND YOU'RE A LESBIAN.
MAYBE THEY MEANT THESPIAN, HUH?
GO AWAY, JOHNNY.
BUT I STUCK UP FOR YA'. NO WAY SHE'S A DYKE, I SAID. NOT MY GIRL! I GOT THE TEETH MARKS TO PROVE IT, DON'T I BABE?
DON'T SCREW WITH ME, JOHNNY. I'M NOT IN THE MOOD.
THAT'S FUNNY. THAT'S WHAT YOU SAID LAST WEEK! AND THE WEEK BEFORE THAT, AND THE WEEK BEFORE THAT...
SO, WHAT DOES IT TAKE TO GET YOU IN THE MOOD THESE DAYS, CHOOVANSKI?
LISA RILEY?
WHAT'S GOING ON UP THERE? WHO IS THAT?!
YOU'RE DEAD MEAT! YOU HEAR ME?
YOU'RE DEAD!
DYKE!!

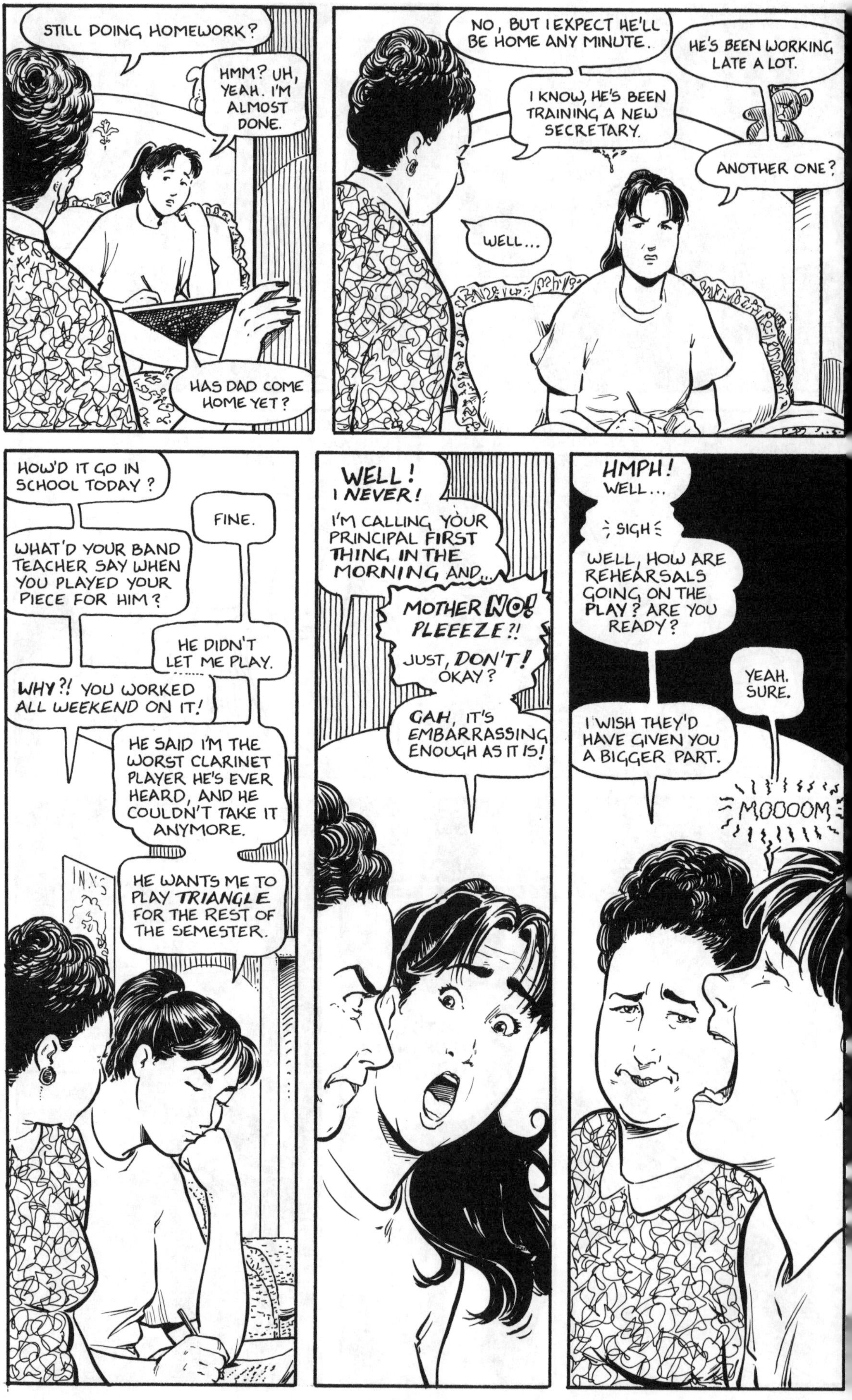

STILL DOING HOMEWORK?
HMM? UH, YEAH. I'M ALMOST DONE.
HAS DAD COME HOME YET?
NO, BUT I EXPECT HE'LL BE HOME ANY MINUTE.
I KNOW, HE'S BEEN TRAINING A NEW SECRETARY.
HE'S BEEN WORKING LATE A LOT.
ANOTHER ONE?
WELL...
HOW'D IT GO IN SCHOOL TODAY?
FINE.
WHAT'D YOUR BAND TEACHER SAY WHEN YOU PLAYED YOUR PIECE FOR HIM?
HE DIDN'T LET ME PLAY.
WHY?! YOU WORKED ALL WEEKEND ON IT!
HE SAID I'M THE WORST CLARINET PLAYER HE'S EVER HEARD, AND HE COULDN'T TAKE IT ANYMORE.
HE WANTS ME TO PLAY TRIANGLE FOR THE REST OF THE SEMESTER.
WELL! I NEVER!
I'M CALLING YOUR PRINCIPAL FIRST THING IN THE MORNING AND...
MOTHER NO! PLEEEZE?!
JUST, DON'T! OKAY?
GAH, IT'S EMBARRASSING ENOUGH AS IT IS!
HMPH! WELL...
SIGH
WELL, HOW ARE REHEARSALS GOING ON THE PLAY? ARE YOU READY?
YEAH. SURE.
I WISH THEY'D HAVE GIVEN YOU A BIGGER PART.
MOOOOM

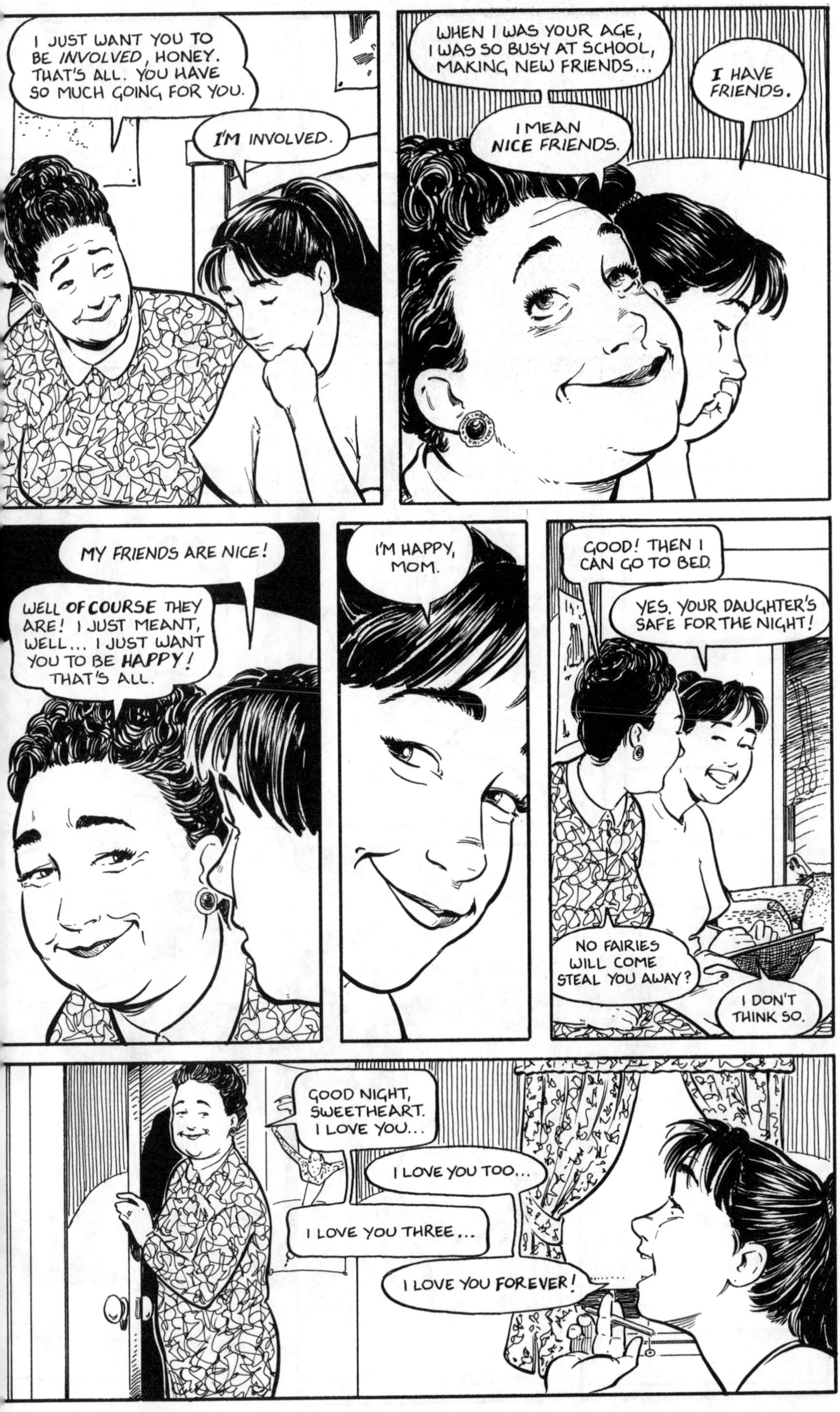
I JUST WANT YOU TO BE INVOLVED, HONEY. THAT'S ALL. YOU HAVE SO MUCH GOING FOR YOU.
I'M INVOLVED.
WHEN I WAS YOUR AGE, I WAS SO BUSY AT SCHOOL, MAKING NEW FRIENDS...
I MEAN NICE FRIENDS.
I HAVE FRIENDS.
MY FRIENDS ARE NICE!
WELL OF COURSE THEY ARE! I JUST MEANT, WELL... I JUST WANT YOU TO BE HAPPY! THAT'S ALL.
I'M HAPPY, MOM.
GOOD! THEN I CAN GO TO BED.
YES. YOUR DAUGHTER'S SAFE FOR THE NIGHT!
NO FAIRIES WILL COME STEAL YOU AWAY?
I DON'T THINK SO.
GOOD NIGHT, SWEETHEART. I LOVE YOU...
I LOVE YOU TOO...
I LOVE YOU THREE...
I LOVE YOU FOREVER!

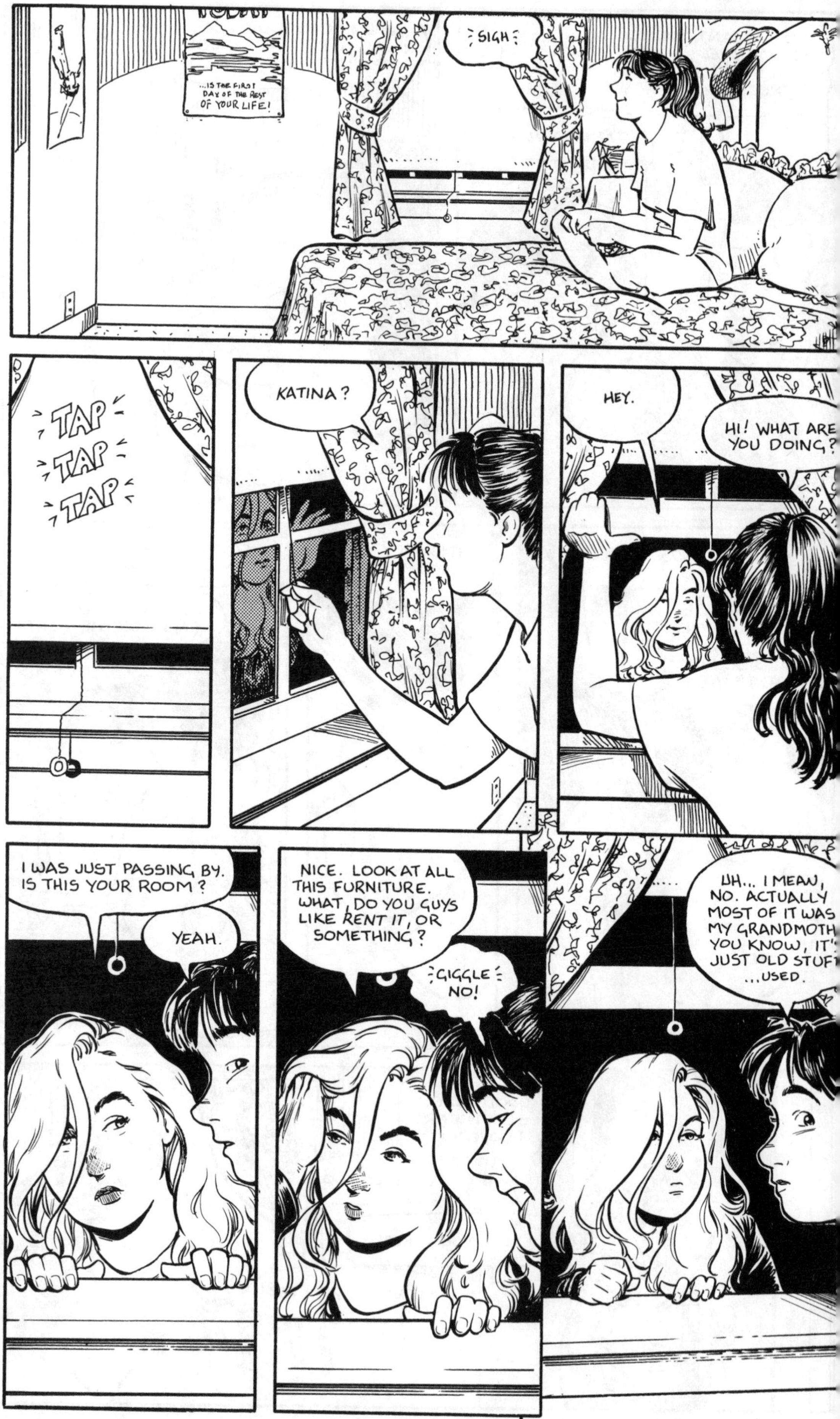
...IS THE FIRST DAY OF THE REST OF YOUR LIFE!
SIGH
TAP TAP TAP
KATINA?
HEY.
HI! WHAT ARE YOU DOING?
I WAS JUST PASSING BY. IS THIS YOUR ROOM?
YEAH.
NICE. LOOK AT ALL THIS FURNITURE. WHAT, DO YOU GUYS LIKE RENT IT, OR SOMETHING?
GIGGLE NO!
UH... I MEAN, NO. ACTUALLY MOST OF IT WAS MY GRANDMOTH YOU KNOW, IT' JUST OLD STUF ...USED.

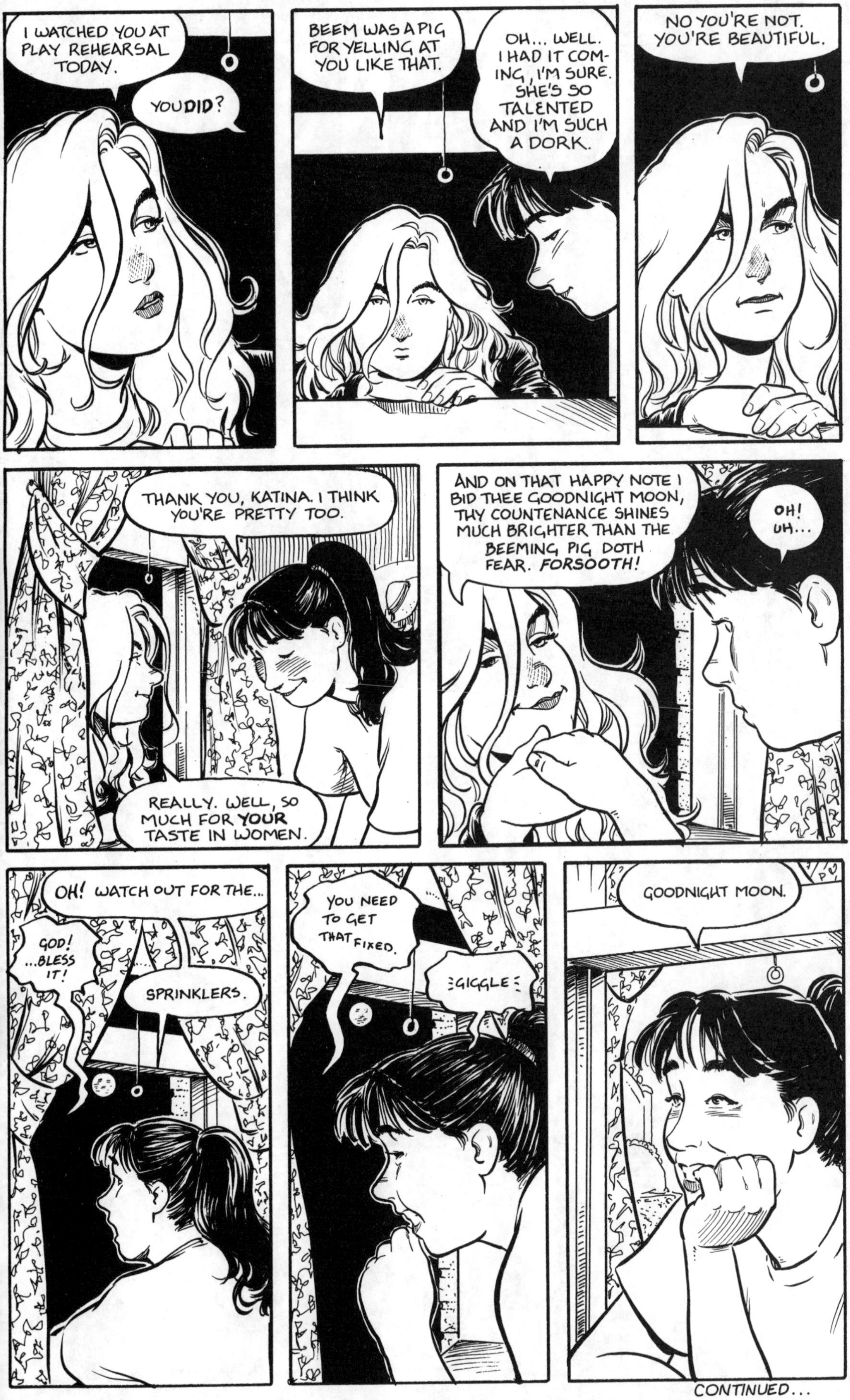
I WATCHED YOU AT PLAY REHEARSAL TODAY.
YOU DID?
BEEM WAS A PIG FOR YELLING AT YOU LIKE THAT.
OH... WELL. I HAD IT COMING, I'M SURE. SHE'S SO TALENTED AND I'M SUCH A DORK.
NO YOU'RE NOT. YOU'RE BEAUTIFUL.
THANK YOU, KATINA. I THINK YOU'RE PRETTY TOO.
REALLY. WELL, SO MUCH FOR YOUR TASTE IN WOMEN.
AND ON THAT HAPPY NOTE I BID THEE GOODNIGHT MOON, THY COUNTENANCE SHINES MUCH BRIGHTER THAN THE BEEMING PIG DOTH FEAR. FORSOOTH!
OH! UH...
OH! WATCH OUT FOR THE...
GOD! ...BLESS IT!
SPRINKLERS.
YOU NEED TO GET THAT FIXED.
GIGGLE
GOODNIGHT MOON.

CONTINUED...

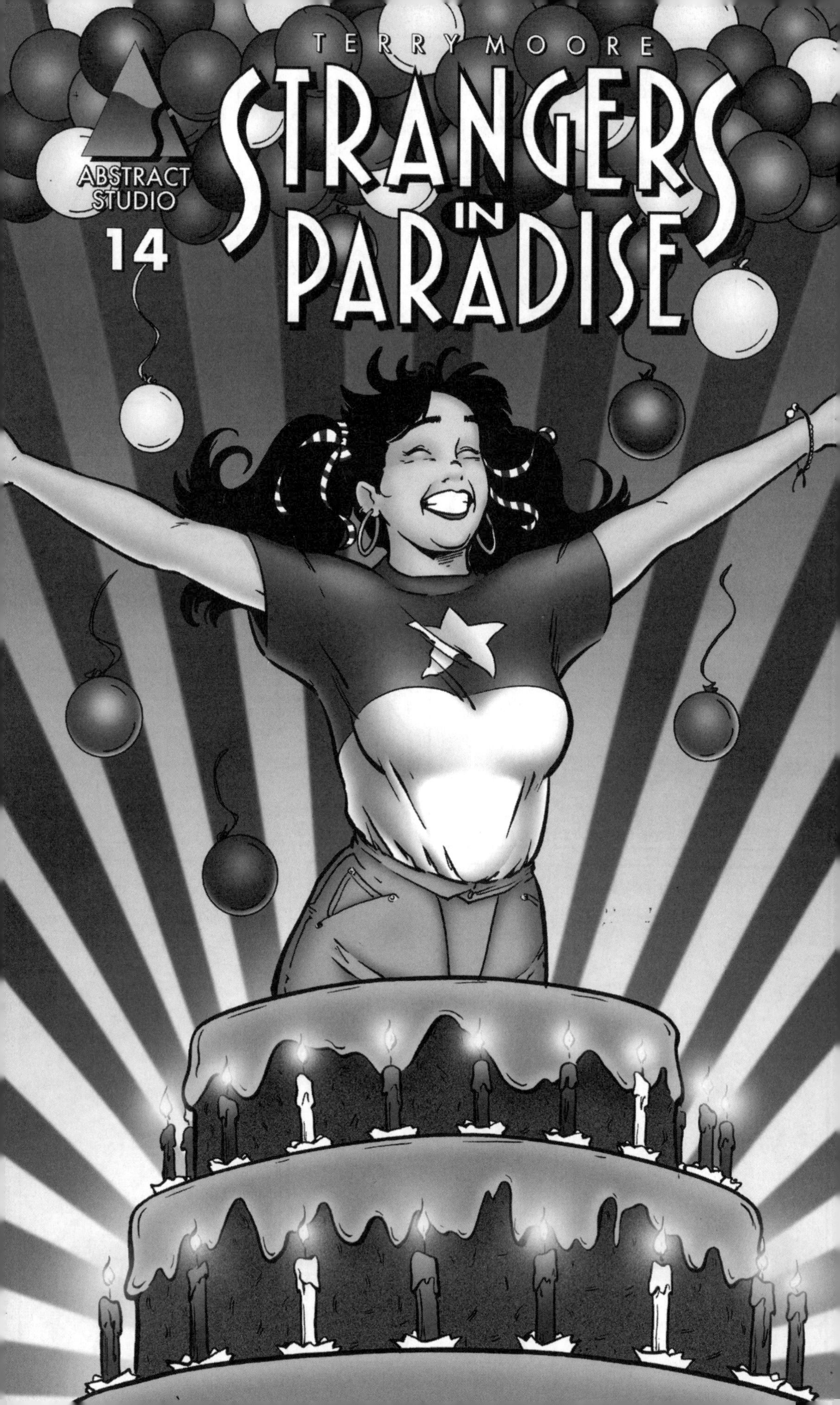
TERRY MOORE
STRANGERS IN PARADISE
ABSTRACT STUDIO
14

Passion Cry

Sitting in a park in the middle of the night
Trying to reason what is wrong from what is right.
I am only as you see me
I am lonely till you free me
I'm a passion cry.

Once and then twice just to twist the knife
You've loved me and left me to figure out
Your fear of night.
When you love me you confuse me
When you're lonely then you use me
Like a sacrifice.

Everyone here has the Christmas cheer
When the snow starts to fall
Wish they'd get on with the brand new year.
With the coming of the seasons
"I'll be gone and you can reason
Why i left you here."
What i need is a start in another town
Where the people are new and musicians
Are playing a whole new sound.
But you call me like a siren
When you know there's something dyin'
Deep inside of me.

Sitting in a park in the middle of the night
Trying to reason what is wrong from what is right.
I am only as you see me
I am lonely till you free me
I'm a passion cry.

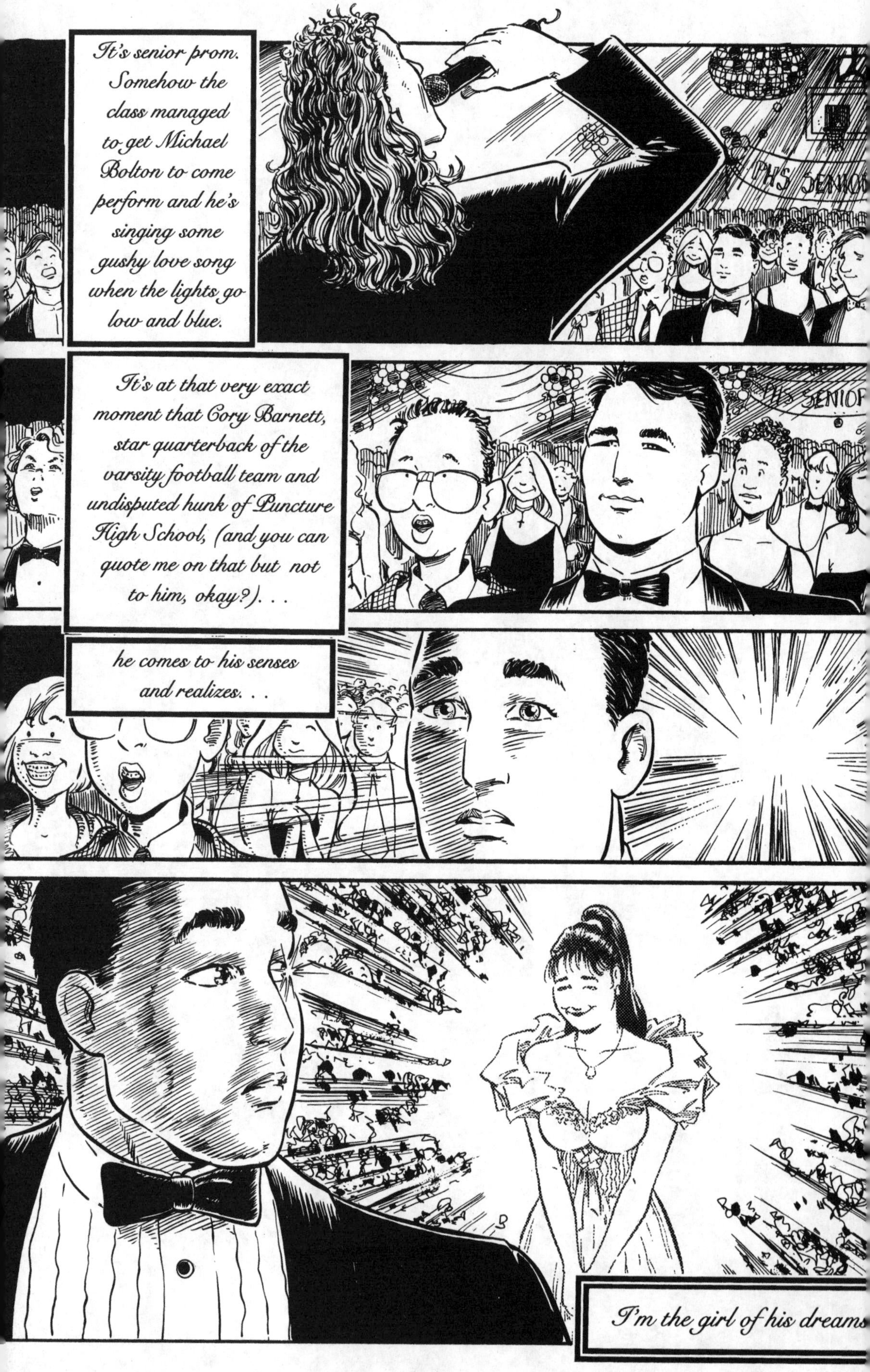
It's senior prom. Somehow the class managed to get Michael Bolton to come perform and he's singing some gushy love song when the lights go low and blue.
PHS SENIOR
It's at that very exact moment that Cory Barnett, star quarterback of the varsity football team and undisputed hunk of Puncture High School, (and you can quote me on that but not to him, okay?). . .
he comes to his senses and realizes. . .
I'm the girl of his dreams

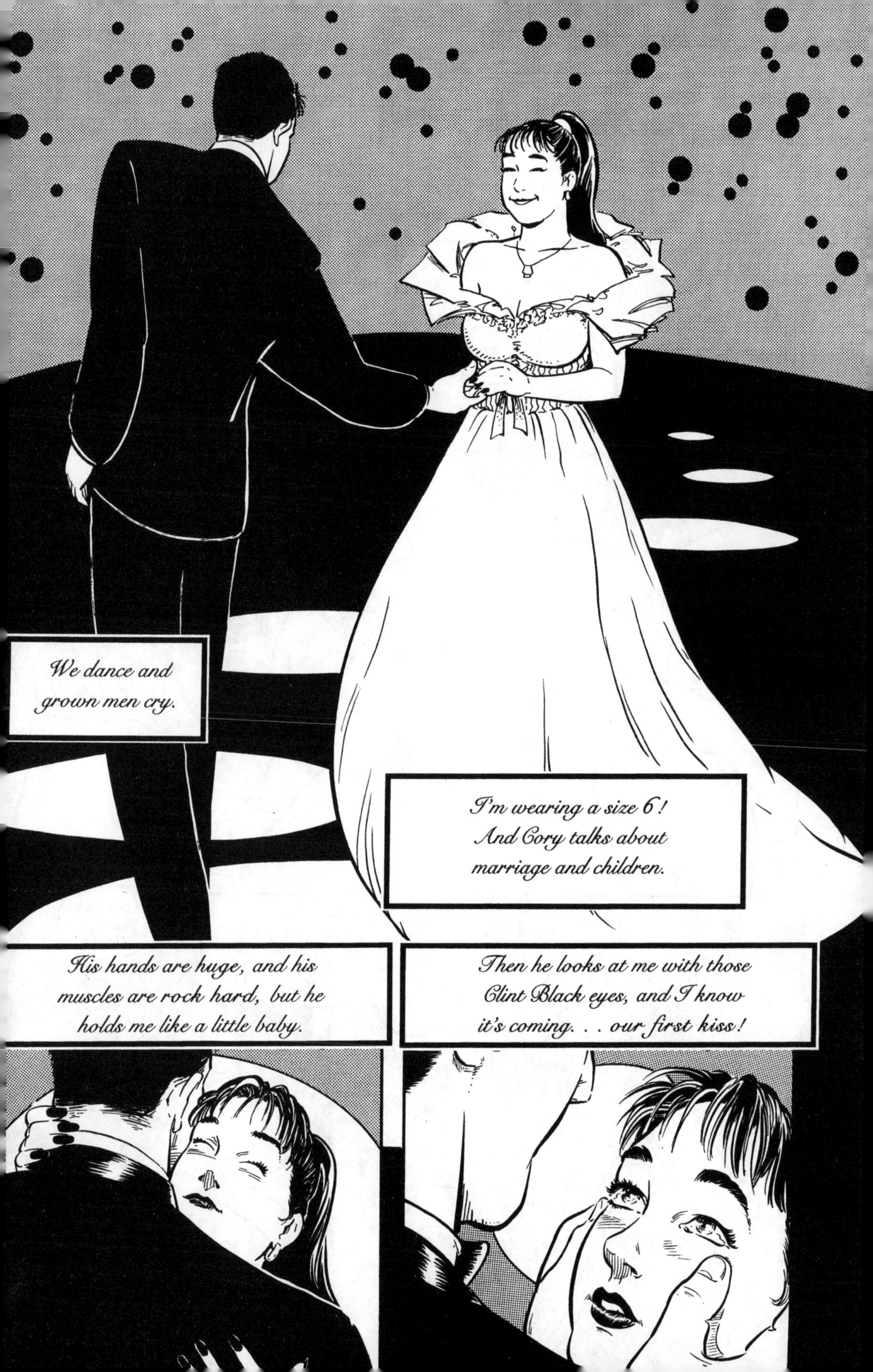

We dance and grown men cry.
I'm wearing a size 6! And Cory talks about marriage and children.
His hands are huge, and his muscles are rock hard, but he holds me like a little baby.
Then he looks at me with those Clint Black eyes, and I know it's coming. . . our first kiss!

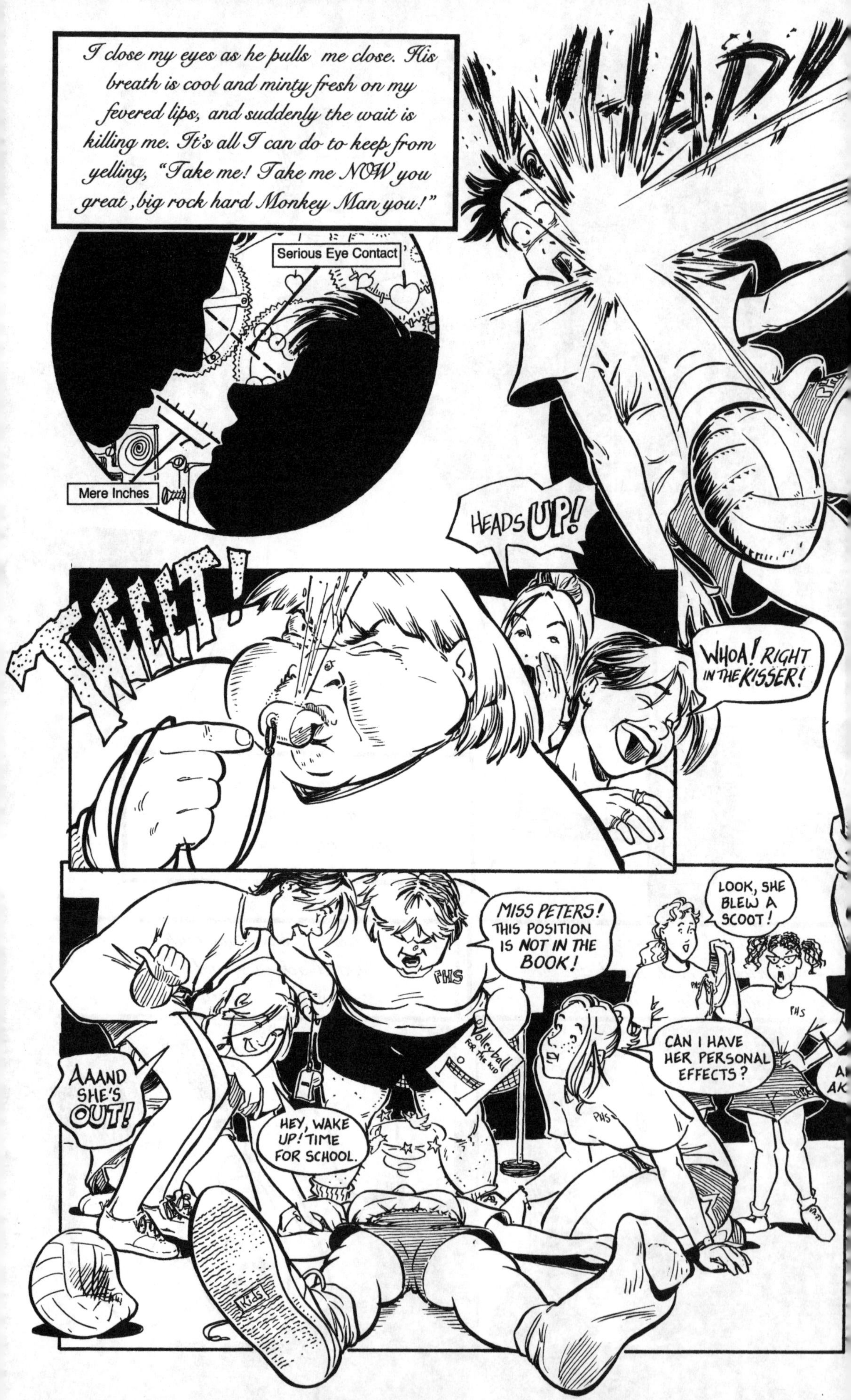
I close my eyes as he pulls me close. His breath is cool and minty fresh on my fevered lips, and suddenly the wait is killing me. It's all I can do to keep from yelling, "Take me! Take me NOW you great ,big rock hard Monkey Man you!"
Serious Eye Contact
Mere Inches
WHAP!
HEADS UP!
TWEET!
WHOA! RIGHT IN THE KISSER!
MISS PETERS! THIS POSITION IS NOT IN THE BOOK!
LOOK, SHE BLEW A SCOOT!
CAN I HAVE HER PERSONAL EFFECTS?
AAAND SHE'S OUT!
HEY, WAKE UP! TIME FOR SCHOOL.
Volleyball FOR THE KID
PHS

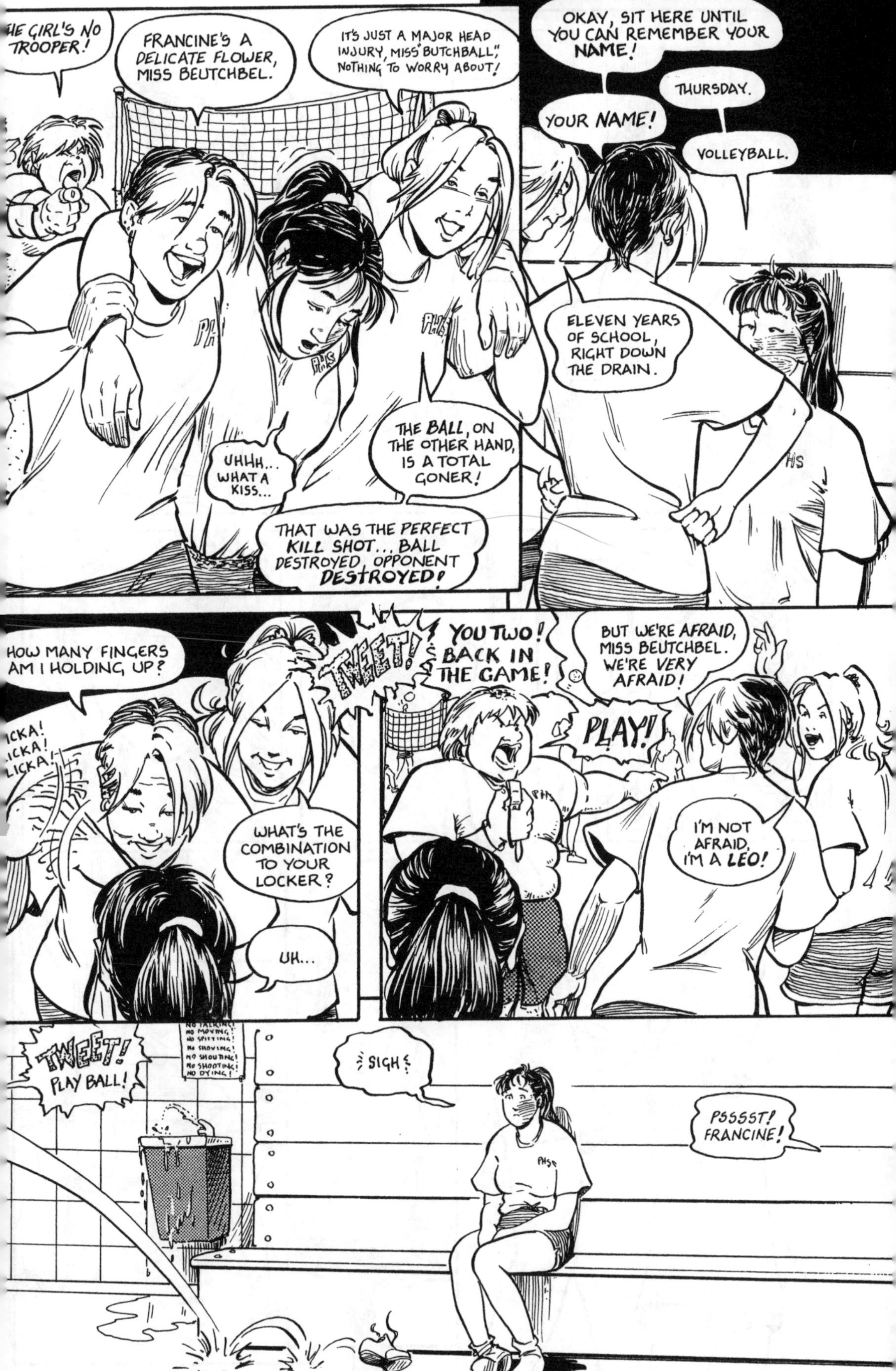
HE GIRL'S NO TROOPER!
FRANCINE'S A DELICATE FLOWER, MISS BEUTCHBEL.
IT'S JUST A MAJOR HEAD INJURY, MISS "BUTCHBALL," NOTHING TO WORRY ABOUT!
UHHH... WHAT A KISS...
THE BALL, ON THE OTHER HAND, IS A TOTAL GONER!
THAT WAS THE PERFECT KILL SHOT... BALL DESTROYED OPPONENT DESTROYED!
OKAY, SIT HERE UNTIL YOU CAN REMEMBER YOUR NAME!
YOUR NAME!
THURSDAY.
VOLLEYBALL.
ELEVEN YEARS OF SCHOOL, RIGHT DOWN THE DRAIN.
HOW MANY FINGERS AM I HOLDING UP?
ICKA! ICKA! ICKA!
WHAT'S THE COMBINATION TO YOUR LOCKER?
UH...
TWEET!
YOU TWO! BACK IN THE GAME!
BUT WE'RE AFRAID, MISS BEUTCHBEL. WE'RE VERY AFRAID!
PLAY!
I'M NOT AFRAID, I'M A LEO!
TWEET! PLAY BALL!
NO TALKING! NO MOVING! NO SPITTING! NO SHOVING! NO SHOUTING! NO SHOOTING! NO DYING!
SIGH
PSSSST! FRANCINE!

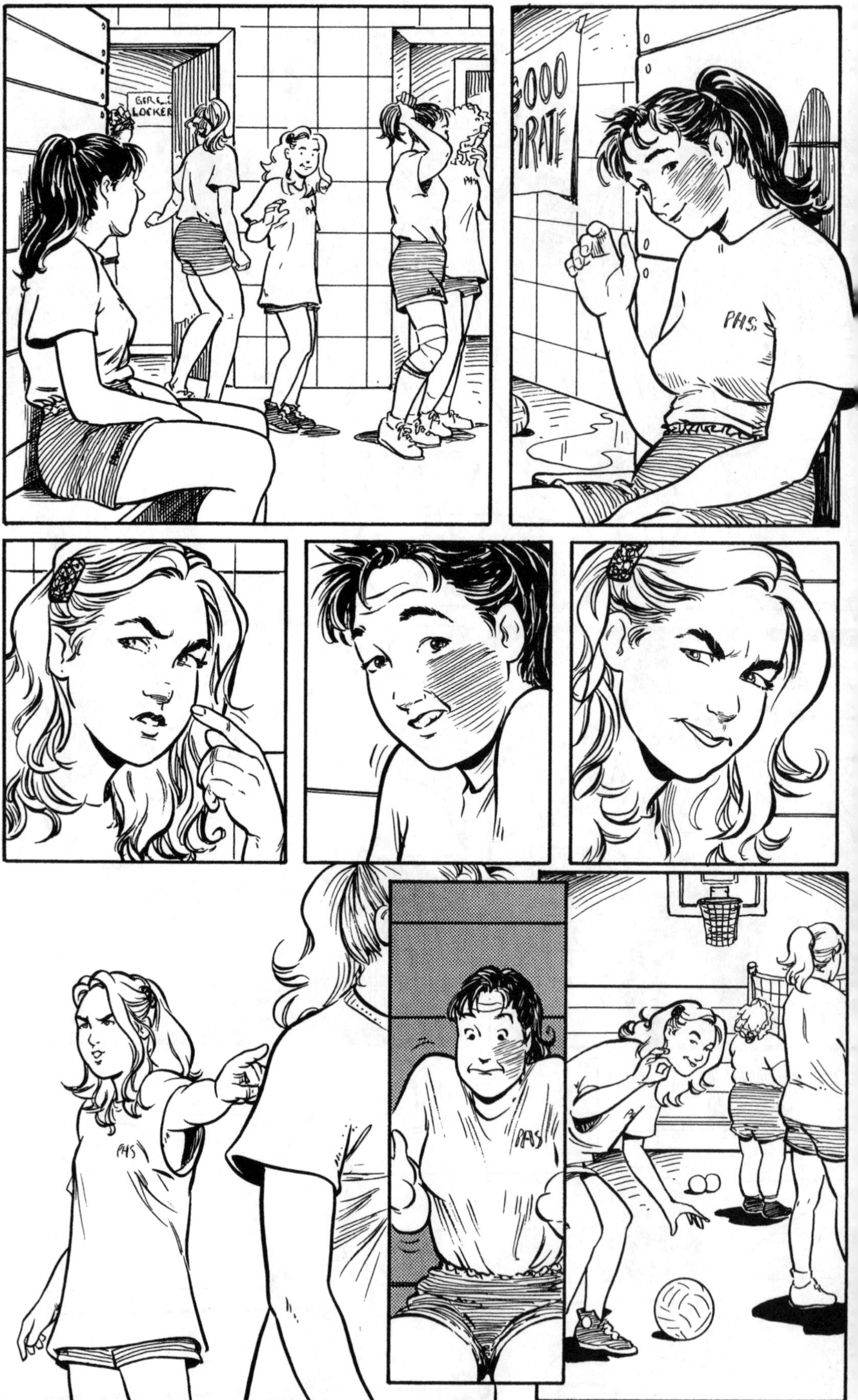
GOOO
PIRATE
PHS

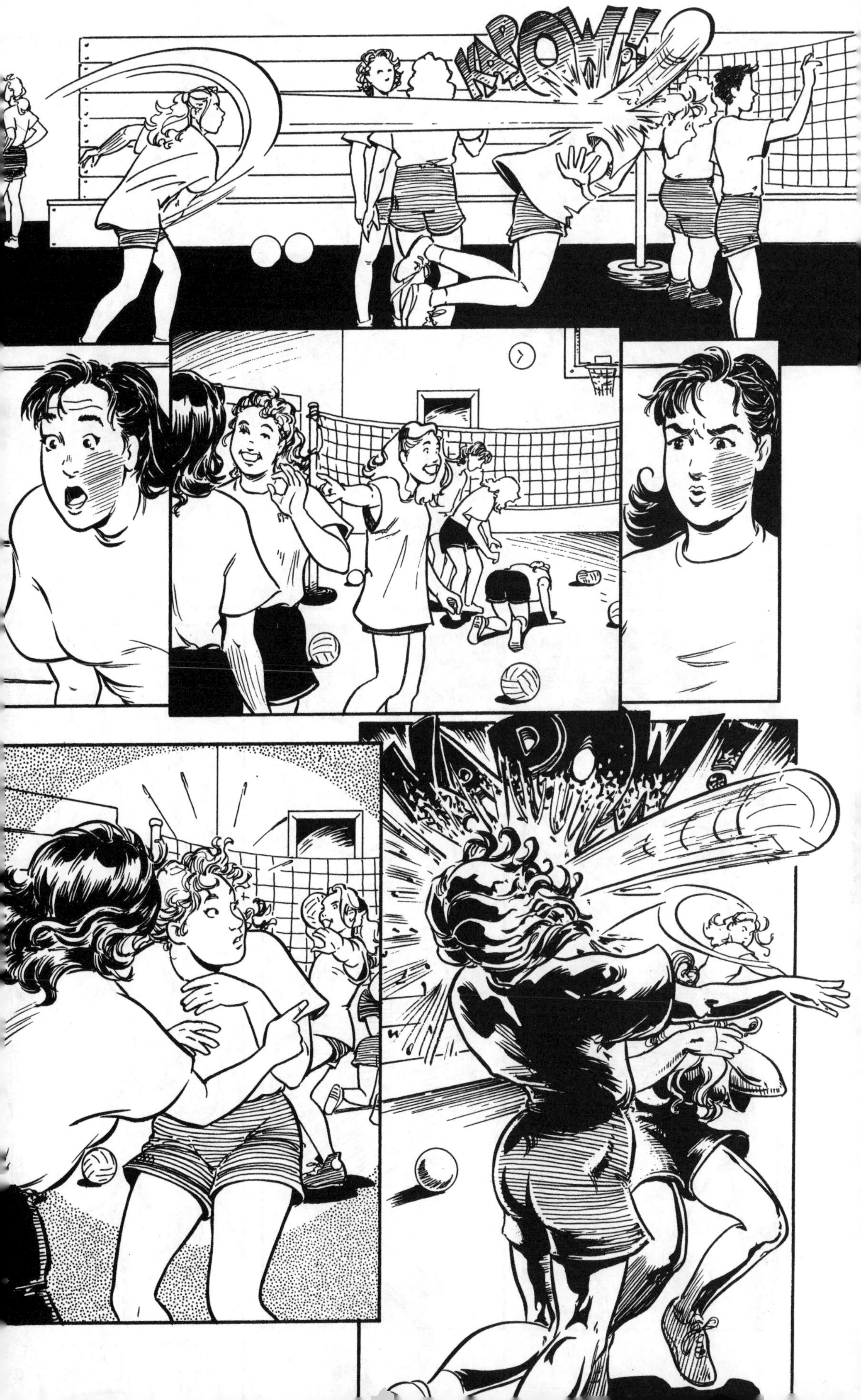
KAPOW!
WAPOW!

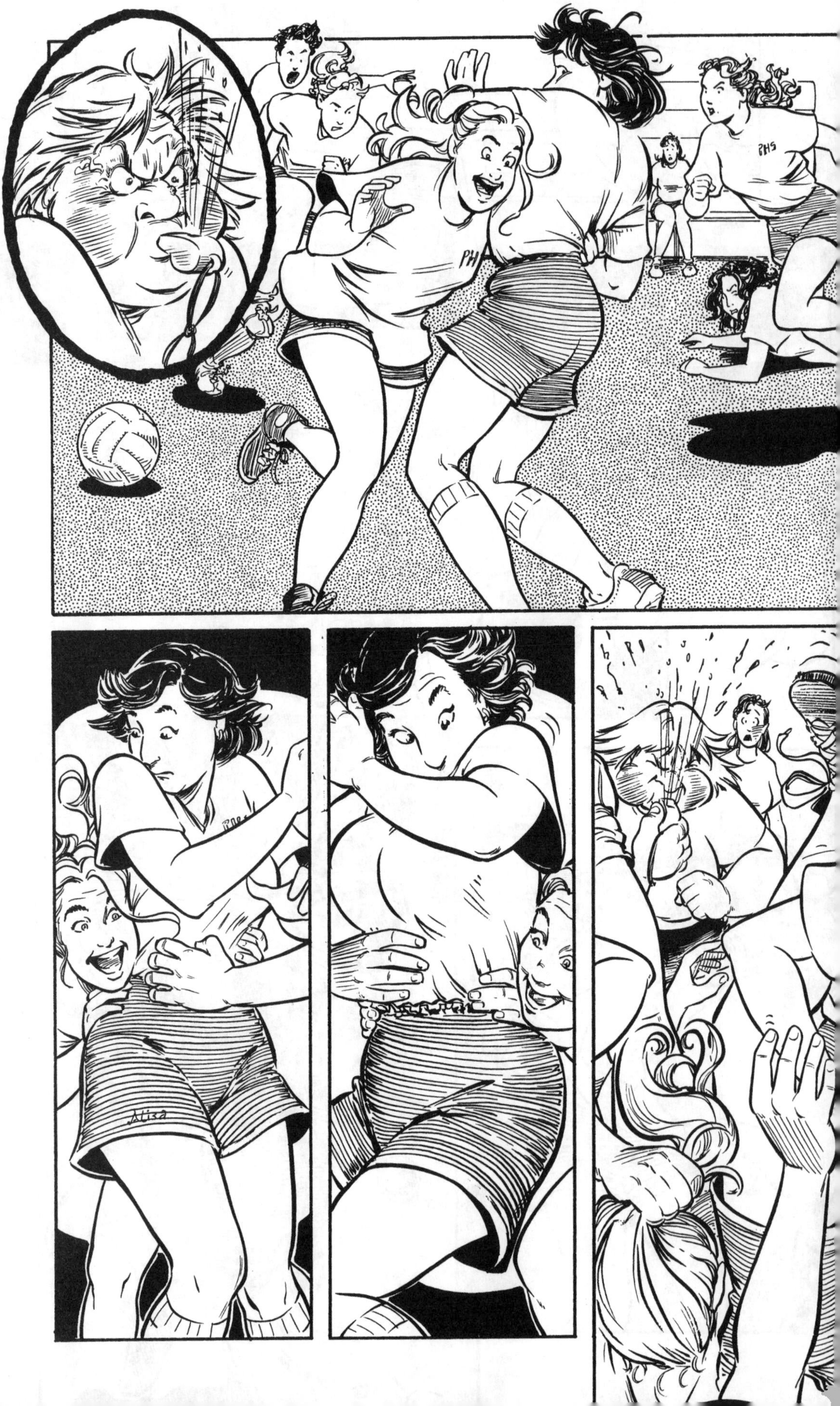
PHS
Alisa

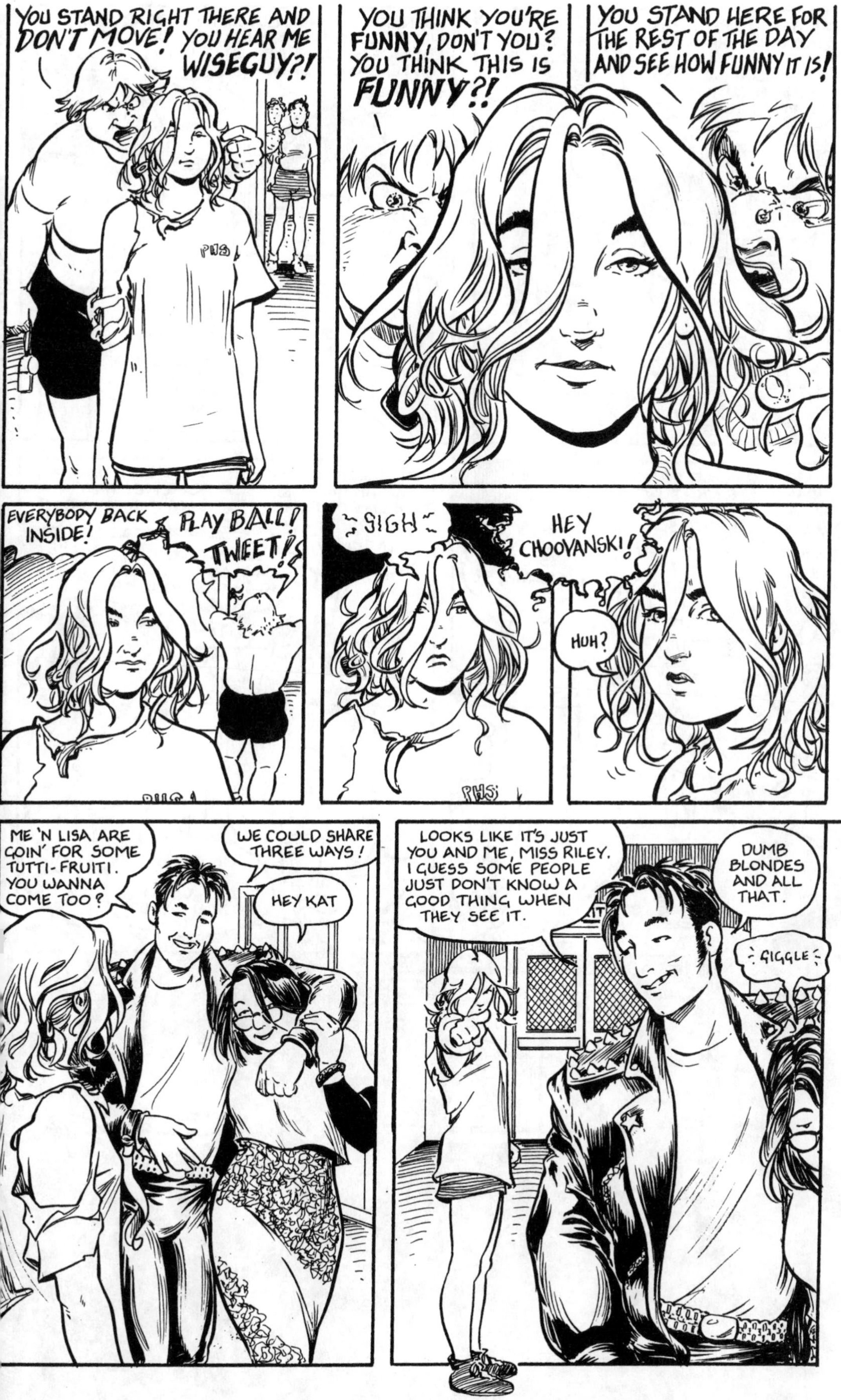

YOU STAND RIGHT THERE AND DON'T MOVE! YOU HEAR ME WISEGUY?!
YOU THINK YOU'RE FUNNY, DON'T YOU? YOU THINK THIS IS FUNNY?!
YOU STAND HERE FOR THE REST OF THE DAY AND SEE HOW FUNNY IT IS!
EVERYBODY BACK INSIDE!
PLAY BALL!
TWEET!
SIGH
HEY CHOOVANSKI!
HUH?
ME 'N LISA ARE GOIN' FOR SOME TUTTI-FRUITI. YOU WANNA COME TOO?
WE COULD SHARE THREE WAYS!
HEY KAT
LOOKS LIKE IT'S JUST YOU AND ME, MISS RILEY. I GUESS SOME PEOPLE JUST DON'T KNOW A GOOD THING WHEN THEY SEE IT.
DUMB BLONDES AND ALL THAT.
GIGGLE

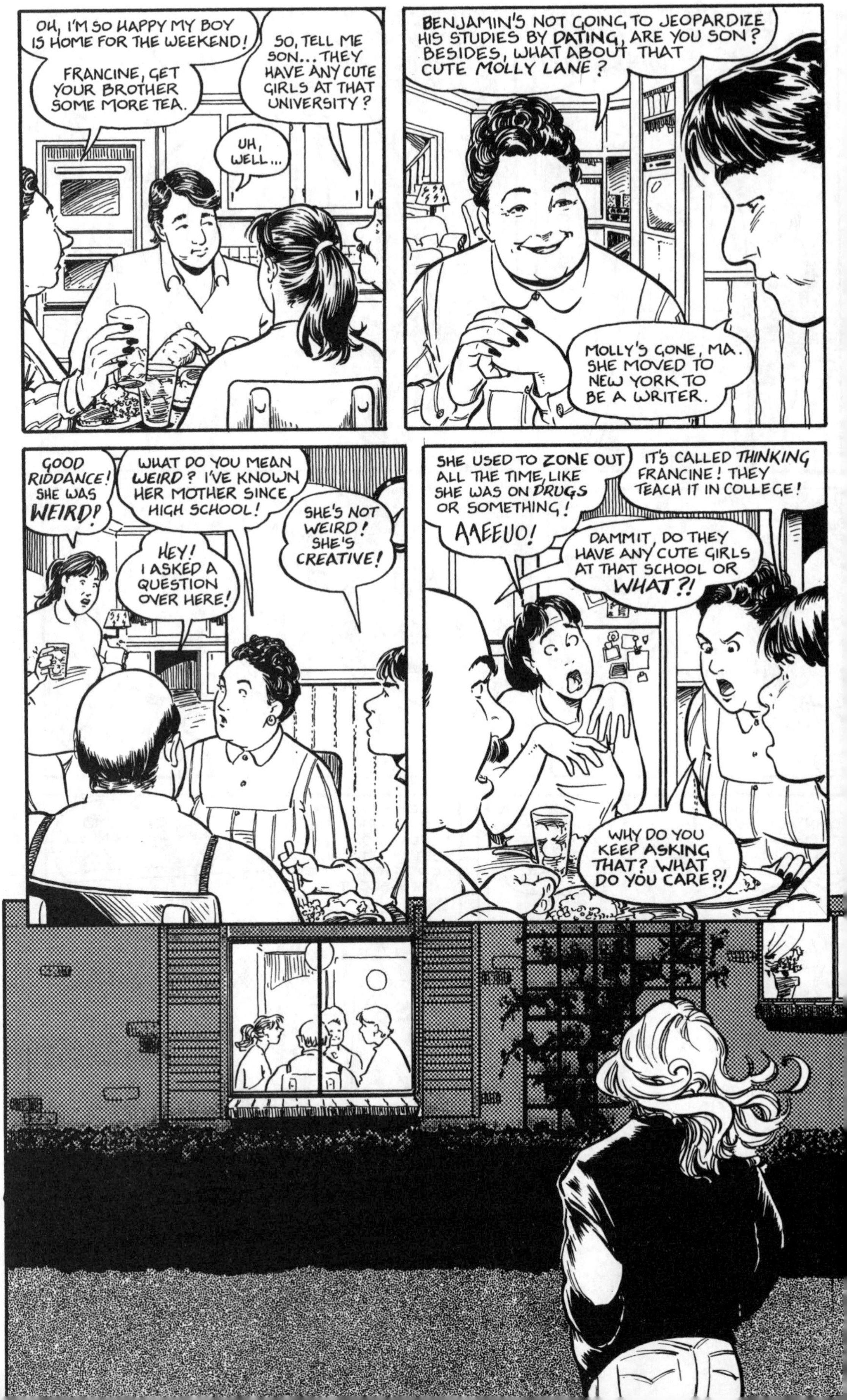

OH, I'M SO HAPPY MY BOY IS HOME FOR THE WEEKEND!
FRANCINE, GET YOUR BROTHER SOME MORE TEA.
SO, TELL ME SON... THEY HAVE ANY CUTE GIRLS AT THAT UNIVERSITY?
UH, WELL...
BENJAMIN'S NOT GOING TO JEOPARDIZE HIS STUDIES BY DATING, ARE YOU SON? BESIDES, WHAT ABOUT THAT CUTE MOLLY LANE?
MOLLY'S GONE, MA. SHE MOVED TO NEW YORK TO BE A WRITER.
GOOD RIDDANCE! SHE WAS WEIRD!
WHAT DO YOU MEAN WEIRD? I'VE KNOWN HER MOTHER SINCE HIGH SCHOOL!
HEY! I ASKED A QUESTION OVER HERE!
SHE'S NOT WEIRD! SHE'S CREATIVE!
SHE USED TO ZONE OUT ALL THE TIME, LIKE SHE WAS ON DRUGS OR SOMETHING!
AAEEUO!
IT'S CALLED THINKING FRANCINE! THEY TEACH IT IN COLLEGE!
DAMMIT, DO THEY HAVE ANY CUTE GIRLS AT THAT SCHOOL OR WHAT?!
WHY DO YOU KEEP ASKING THAT? WHAT DO YOU CARE?!

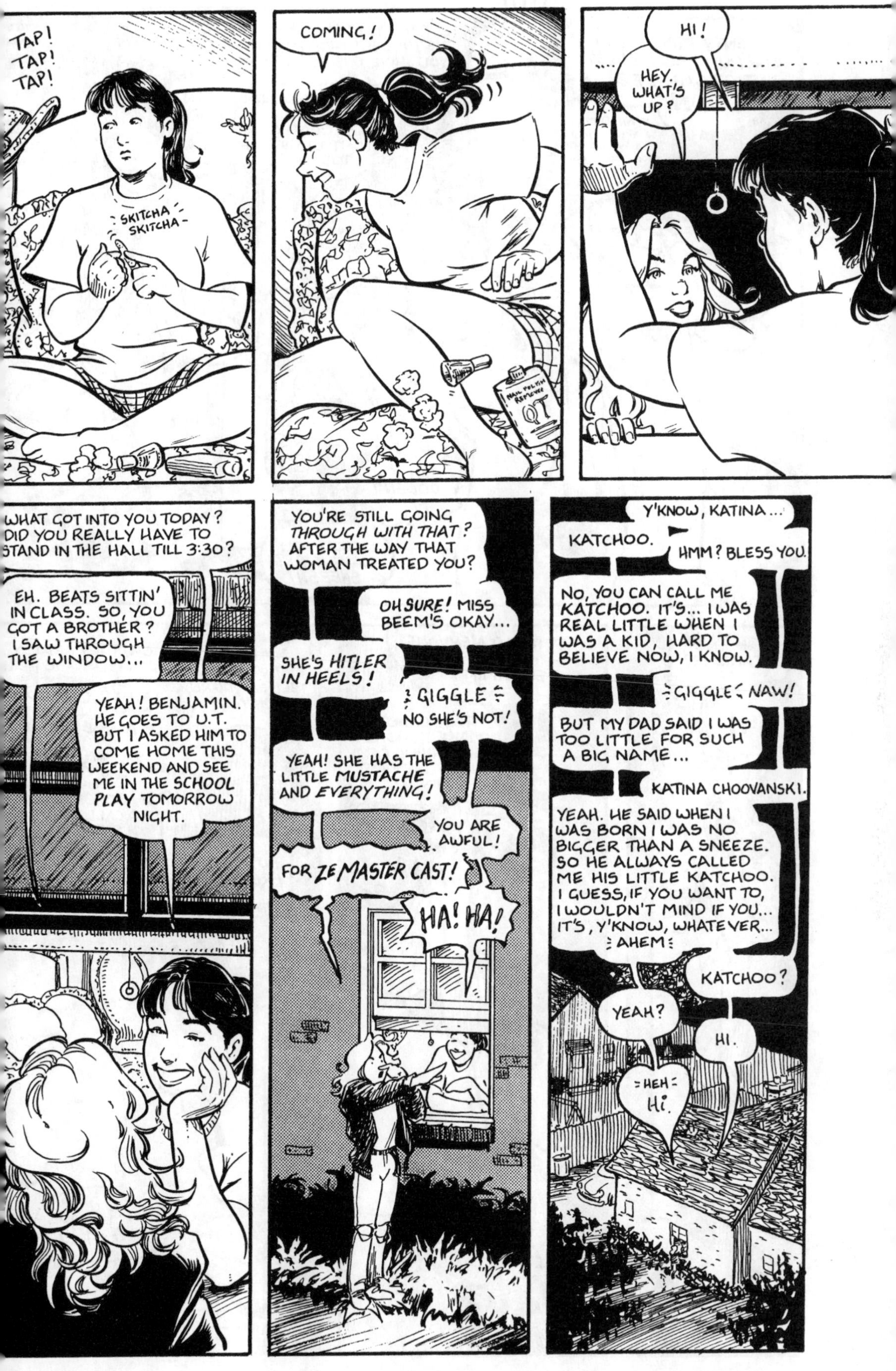

TAP! TAP! TAP!
SKITCHA SKITCHA
COMING!
HI!
HEY. WHAT'S UP?
WHAT GOT INTO YOU TODAY? DID YOU REALLY HAVE TO STAND IN THE HALL TILL 3:30?
EH. BEATS SITTIN' IN CLASS. SO, YOU GOT A BROTHER? I SAW THROUGH THE WINDOW...
YEAH! BENJAMIN. HE GOES TO U.T. BUT I ASKED HIM TO COME HOME THIS WEEKEND AND SEE ME IN THE SCHOOL PLAY TOMORROW NIGHT.
YOU'RE STILL GOING THROUGH WITH THAT? AFTER THE WAY THAT WOMAN TREATED YOU?
OH SURE! MISS BEEM'S OKAY...
SHE'S HITLER IN HEELS!
GIGGLE NO SHE'S NOT!
YEAH! SHE HAS THE LITTLE MUSTACHE AND EVERYTHING!
YOU ARE AWFUL!
FOR ZE MASTER CAST!
HA! HA!
Y'KNOW, KATINA...
KATCHOO.
HMM? BLESS YOU.
NO, YOU CAN CALL ME KATCHOO. IT'S... I WAS REAL LITTLE WHEN I WAS A KID, HARD TO BELIEVE NOW, I KNOW.
GIGGLE NAW!
BUT MY DAD SAID I WAS TOO LITTLE FOR SUCH A BIG NAME...
KATINA CHOOVANSKI.
YEAH. HE SAID WHEN I WAS BORN I WAS NO BIGGER THAN A SNEEZE. SO HE ALWAYS CALLED ME HIS LITTLE KATCHOO. I GUESS, IF YOU WANT TO, I WOULDN'T MIND IF YOU... IT'S, Y'KNOW, WHATEVER... AHEM
KATCHOO?
YEAH?
HI.
HEH Hi.

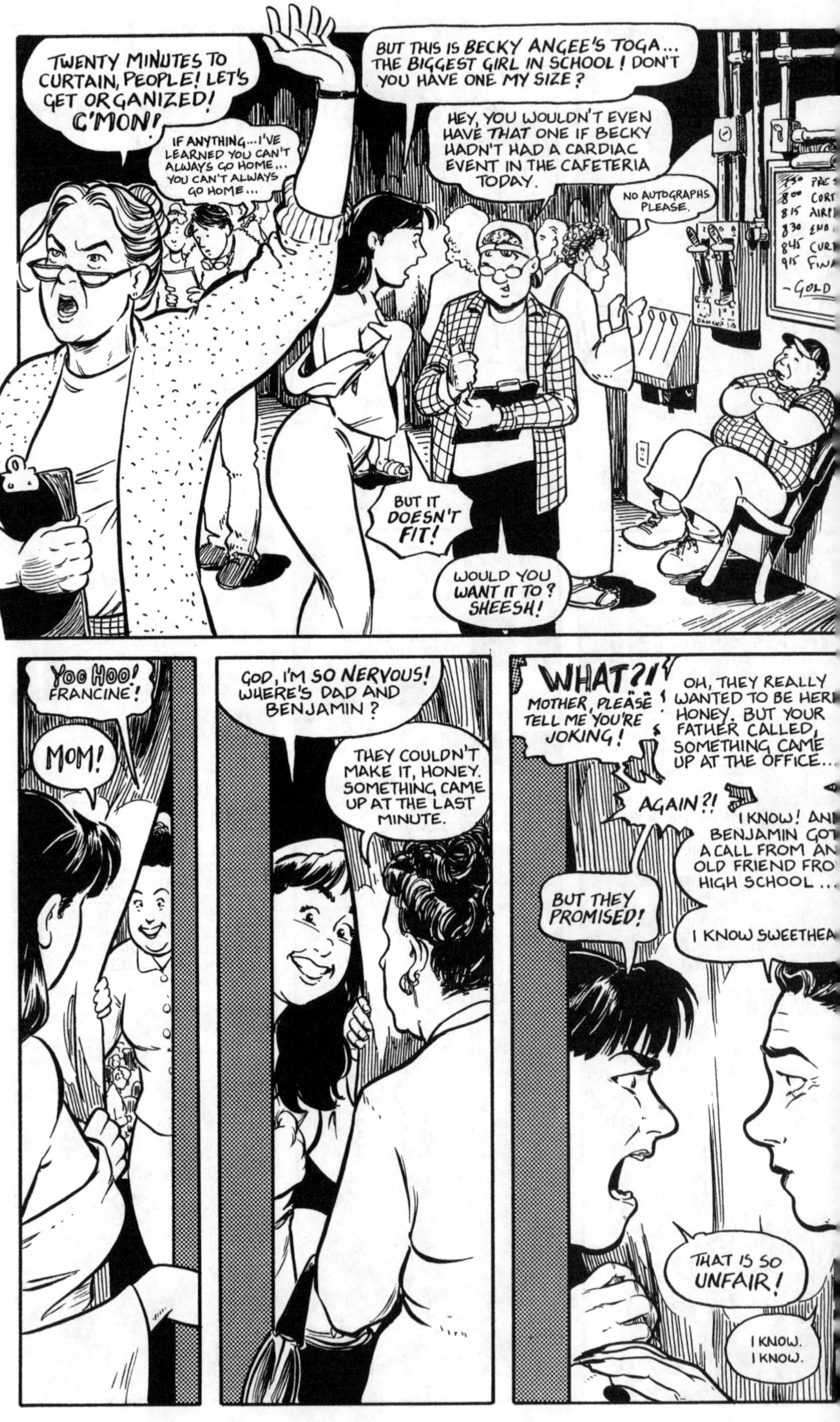

TWENTY MINUTES TO CURTAIN, PEOPLE! LET'S GET ORGANIZED! C'MON!
IF ANYTHING...I'VE LEARNED YOU CAN'T ALWAYS GO HOME... YOU CAN'T ALWAYS GO HOME...
BUT THIS IS BECKY ANGEE'S TOGA... THE BIGGEST GIRL IN SCHOOL! DON'T YOU HAVE ONE MY SIZE?
HEY, YOU WOULDN'T EVEN HAVE THAT ONE IF BECKY HADN'T HAD A CARDIAC EVENT IN THE CAFETERIA TODAY.
NO AUTOGRAPHS PLEASE.
BUT IT DOESN'T FIT!
WOULD YOU WANT IT TO? SHEESH!
YOO HOO! FRANCINE!
MOM!
GOD, I'M SO NERVOUS! WHERE'S DAD AND BENJAMIN?
THEY COULDN'T MAKE IT, HONEY. SOMETHING CAME UP AT THE LAST MINUTE.
WHAT?!
MOTHER, PLEASE TELL ME YOU'RE JOKING!
OH, THEY REALLY WANTED TO BE HER HONEY. BUT YOUR FATHER CALLED, SOMETHING CAME UP AT THE OFFICE...
AGAIN?!
I KNOW! AN BENJAMIN GO A CALL FROM AN OLD FRIEND FRO HIGH SCHOOL...
BUT THEY PROMISED!
I KNOW SWEETHEA
THAT IS SO UNFAIR!
I KNOW. I KNOW.

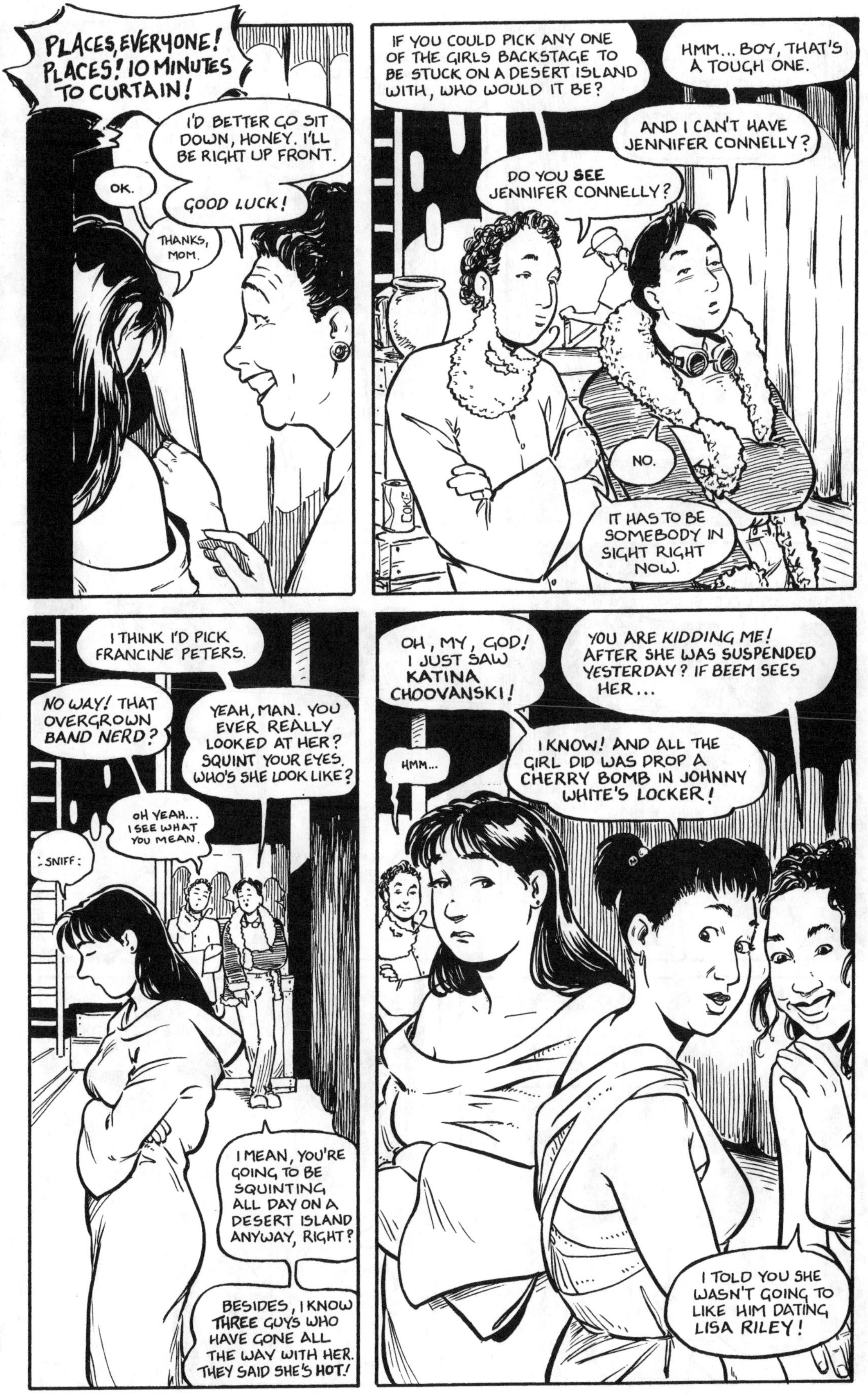
PLACES, EVERYONE! PLACES! 10 MINUTES TO CURTAIN!
I'D BETTER GO SIT DOWN, HONEY. I'LL BE RIGHT UP FRONT.
OK.
GOOD LUCK!
THANKS, MOM.
IF YOU COULD PICK ANY ONE OF THE GIRLS BACKSTAGE TO BE STUCK ON A DESERT ISLAND WITH, WHO WOULD IT BE?
HMM... BOY, THAT'S A TOUGH ONE.
AND I CAN'T HAVE JENNIFER CONNELLY?
DO YOU SEE JENNIFER CONNELLY?
NO.
IT HAS TO BE SOMEBODY IN SIGHT RIGHT NOW.
COKE
I THINK I'D PICK FRANCINE PETERS.
NO WAY! THAT OVERGROWN BAND NERD?
YEAH, MAN. YOU EVER REALLY LOOKED AT HER? SQUINT YOUR EYES. WHO'S SHE LOOK LIKE?
OH YEAH... I SEE WHAT YOU MEAN.
:SNIFF:
I MEAN, YOU'RE GOING TO BE SQUINTING ALL DAY ON A DESERT ISLAND ANYWAY, RIGHT?
BESIDES, I KNOW THREE GUYS WHO HAVE GONE ALL THE WAY WITH HER. THEY SAID SHE'S HOT!
OH, MY, GOD! I JUST SAW KATINA CHOOVANSKI!
YOU ARE KIDDING ME! AFTER SHE WAS SUSPENDED YESTERDAY? IF BEEM SEES HER...
HMM...
I KNOW! AND ALL THE GIRL DID WAS DROP A CHERRY BOMB IN JOHNNY WHITE'S LOCKER!
I TOLD YOU SHE WASN'T GOING TO LIKE HIM DATING LISA RILEY!

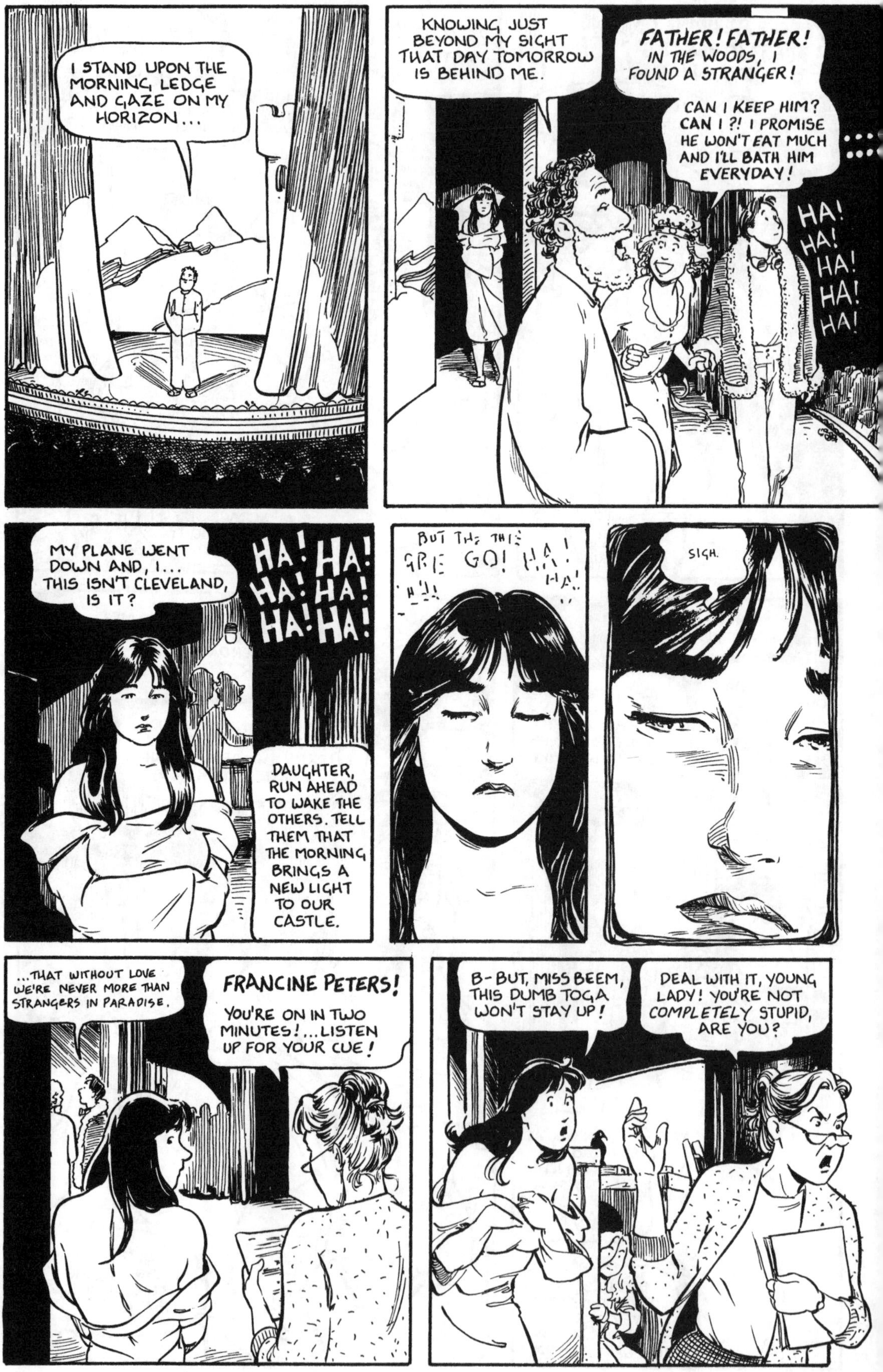
I STAND UPON THE MORNING LEDGE AND GAZE ON MY HORIZON...
KNOWING JUST BEYOND MY SIGHT THAT DAY TOMORROW IS BEHIND ME.
FATHER! FATHER! IN THE WOODS, I FOUND A STRANGER!
CAN I KEEP HIM? CAN I ?! I PROMISE HE WON'T EAT MUCH AND I'LL BATH HIM EVERYDAY!
HA! HA! HA! HA! HA!
MY PLANE WENT DOWN AND, I... THIS ISN'T CLEVELAND, IS IT?
HA! HA! HA! HA! HA! HA!
DAUGHTER, RUN AHEAD TO WAKE THE OTHERS. TELL THEM THAT THE MORNING BRINGS A NEW LIGHT TO OUR CASTLE.
SIGH.
...THAT WITHOUT LOVE WE'RE NEVER MORE THAN STRANGERS IN PARADISE.
FRANCINE PETERS!
YOU'RE ON IN TWO MINUTES!...LISTEN UP FOR YOUR CUE!
B-BUT, MISS BEEM, THIS DUMB TOGA WON'T STAY UP!
DEAL WITH IT, YOUNG LADY! YOU'RE NOT COMPLETELY STUPID, ARE YOU?

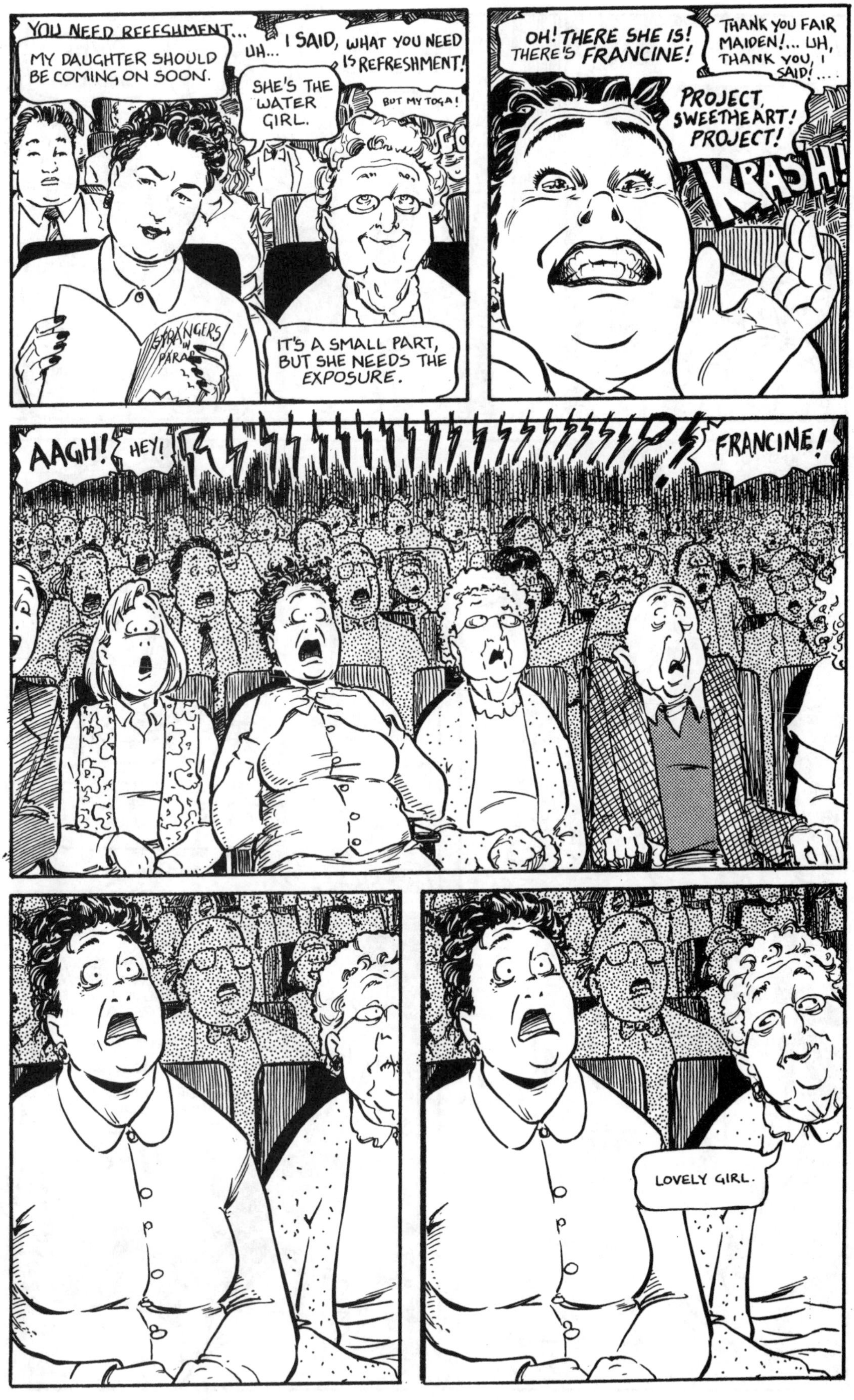
YOU NEED REFFSHMENT...
MY DAUGHTER SHOULD BE COMING ON SOON.
UH... I SAID, WHAT YOU NEED IS REFRESHMENT!
SHE'S THE WATER GIRL.
BUT MY TOGA!
IT'S A SMALL PART, BUT SHE NEEDS THE EXPOSURE.
STRANGERS IN PARA
OH! THERE SHE IS! THERE'S FRANCINE!
THANK YOU FAIR MAIDEN!... UH, THANK YOU, I SAID!...
PROJECT, SWEETHEART! PROJECT!
KRASH!
AAGH!
HEY!
RIIIIIIIIIIIIIIIIIIIP!
FRANCINE!
LOVELY GIRL.

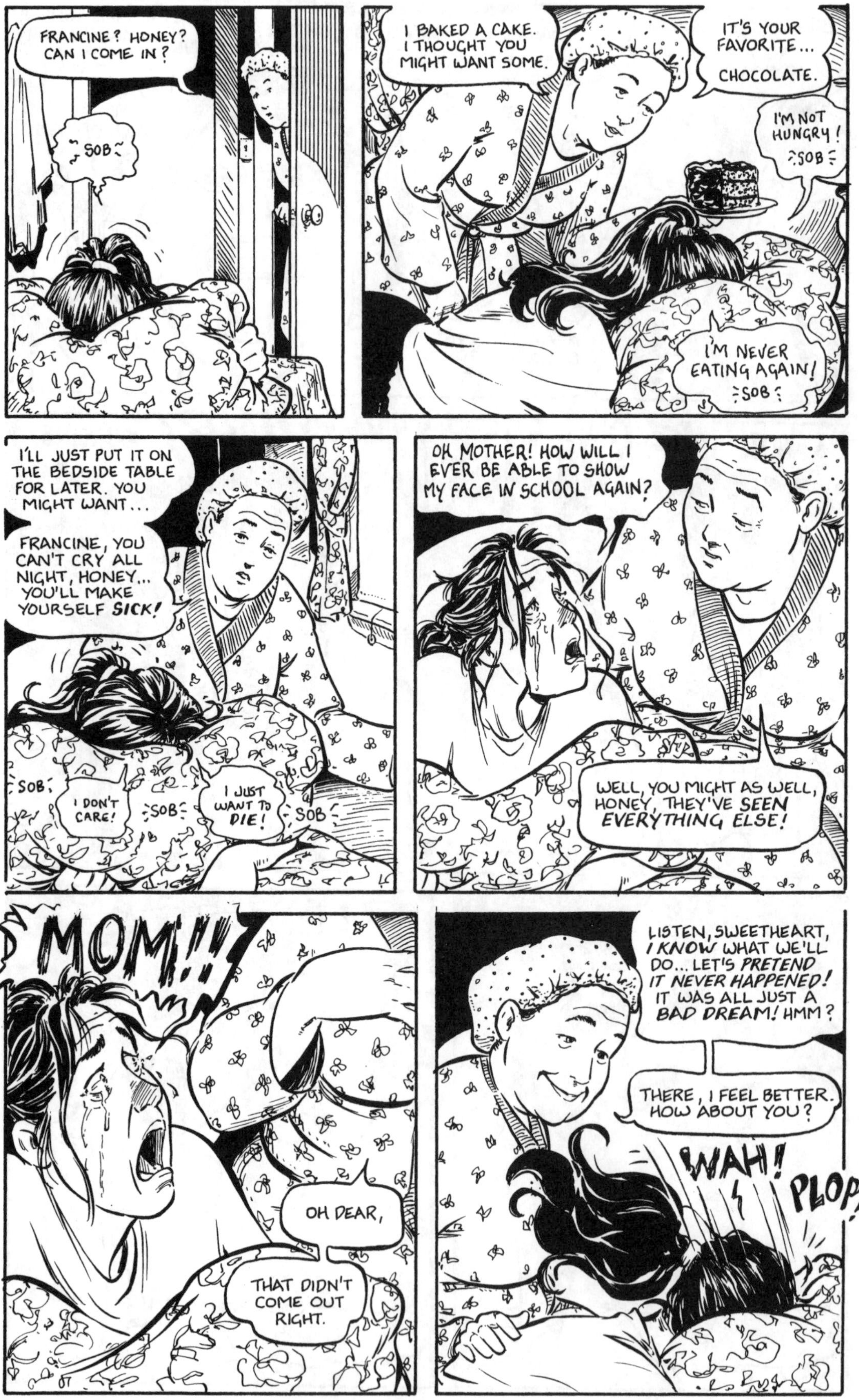
FRANCINE? HONEY? CAN I COME IN?
SOB
I BAKED A CAKE. I THOUGHT YOU MIGHT WANT SOME.
IT'S YOUR FAVORITE... CHOCOLATE.
I'M NOT HUNGRY! SOB
I'M NEVER EATING AGAIN! SOB
I'LL JUST PUT IT ON THE BEDSIDE TABLE FOR LATER. YOU MIGHT WANT...
FRANCINE, YOU CAN'T CRY ALL NIGHT, HONEY... YOU'LL MAKE YOURSELF SICK!
SOB
I DON'T CARE!
SOB
I JUST WANT TO DIE!
SOB
OH MOTHER! HOW WILL I EVER BE ABLE TO SHOW MY FACE IN SCHOOL AGAIN?
WELL, YOU MIGHT AS WELL, HONEY, THEY'VE SEEN EVERYTHING ELSE!
MOM!!!
OH DEAR,
THAT DIDN'T COME OUT RIGHT.
LISTEN, SWEETHEART, I KNOW WHAT WE'LL DO... LET'S PRETEND IT NEVER HAPPENED! IT WAS ALL JUST A BAD DREAM! HMM?
THERE, I FEEL BETTER. HOW ABOUT YOU?
WAH!
PLOP!

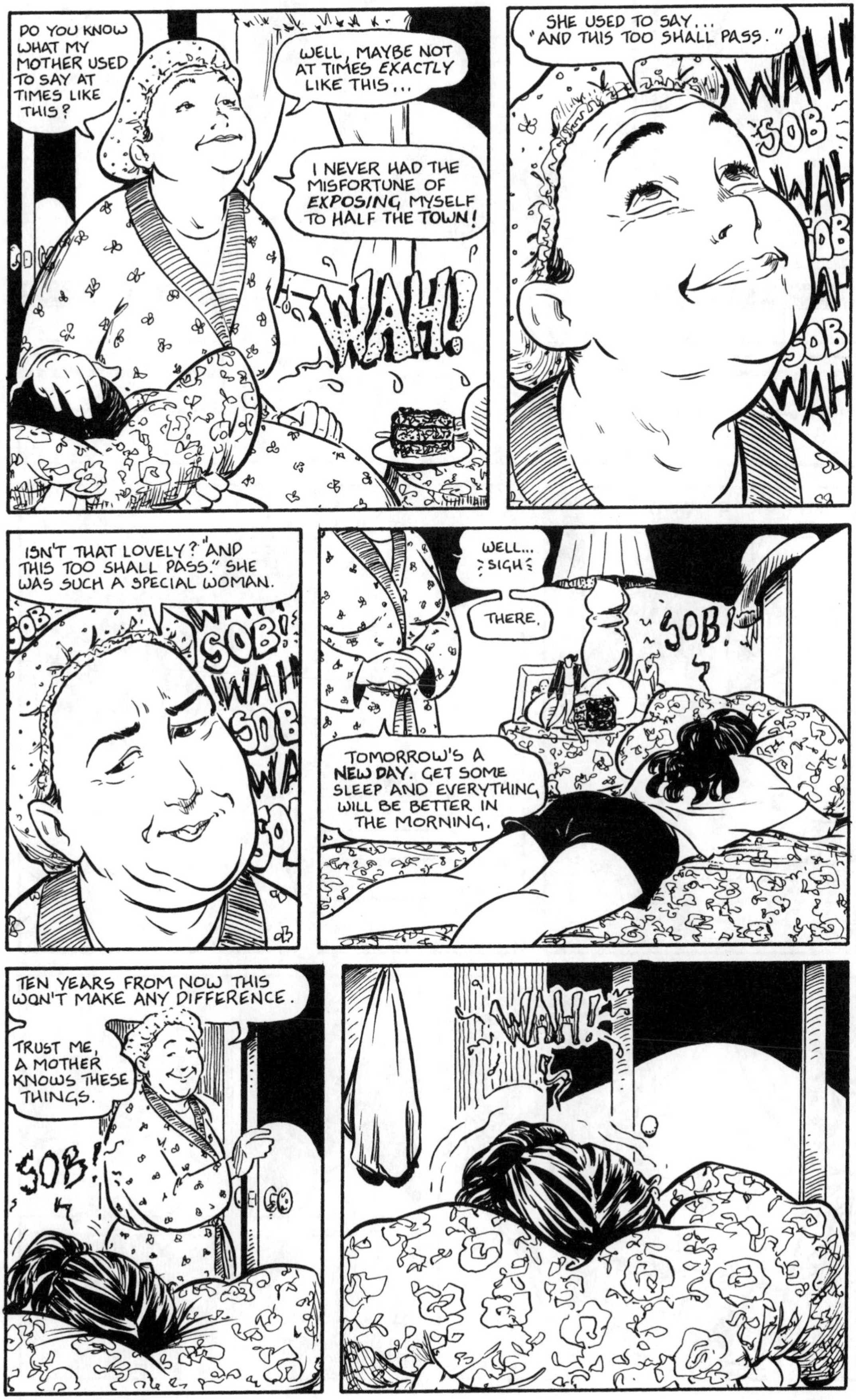
DO YOU KNOW WHAT MY MOTHER USED TO SAY AT TIMES LIKE THIS?
WELL, MAYBE NOT AT TIMES EXACTLY LIKE THIS...
I NEVER HAD THE MISFORTUNE OF EXPOSING MYSELF TO HALF THE TOWN!
WAH!
SHE USED TO SAY... "AND THIS TOO SHALL PASS."
WAH!
SOB
WAH
SOB
WAH
SOB
WAH
ISN'T THAT LOVELY? "AND THIS TOO SHALL PASS." SHE WAS SUCH A SPECIAL WOMAN.
SOB!
WAH
SOB
WELL... SIGH
THERE.
SOB!
TOMORROW'S A NEW DAY. GET SOME SLEEP AND EVERYTHING WILL BE BETTER IN THE MORNING.
TEN YEARS FROM NOW THIS WON'T MAKE ANY DIFFERENCE.
TRUST ME, A MOTHER KNOWS THESE THINGS.
SOB!
WAH!

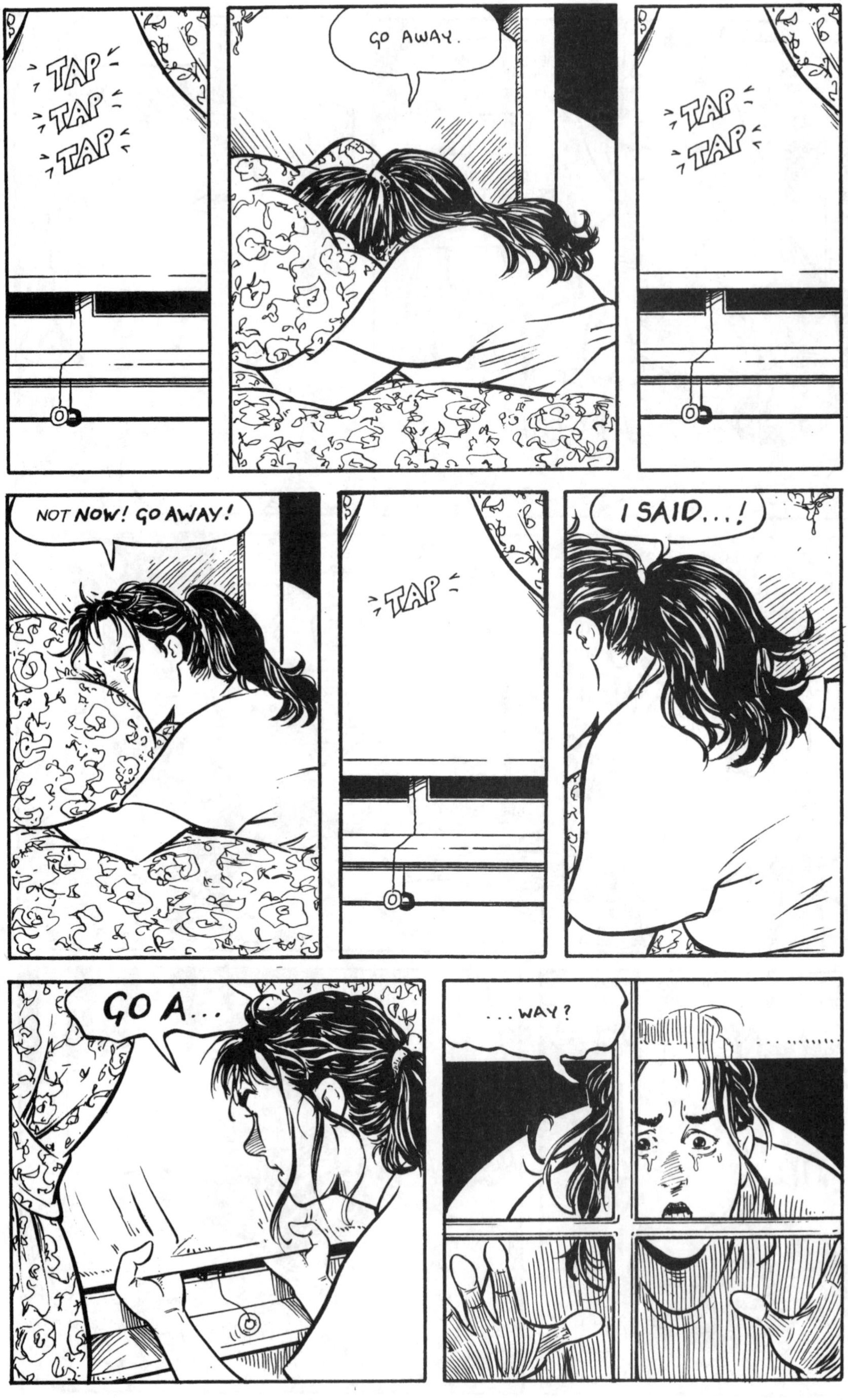
TAP
TAP
TAP
GO AWAY.
TAP
TAP
NOT NOW! GO AWAY!
TAP
I SAID...!
GO A...
...WAY?

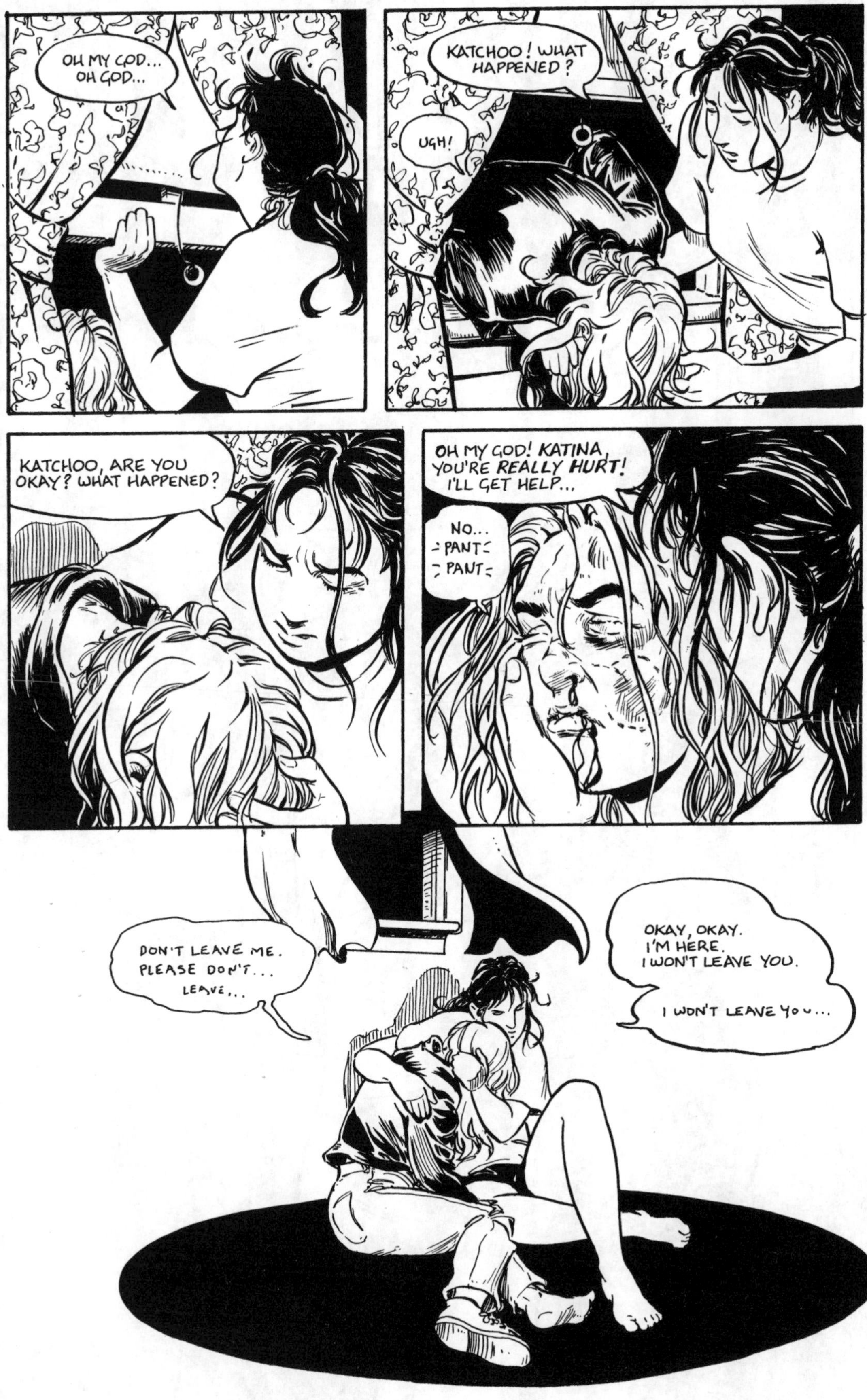
OH MY GOD... OH GOD...
KATCHOO! WHAT HAPPENED?
UGH!
KATCHOO, ARE YOU OKAY? WHAT HAPPENED?
OH MY GOD! KATINA, YOU'RE REALLY HURT! I'LL GET HELP...
NO... PANT PANT
DON'T LEAVE ME. PLEASE DON'T... LEAVE...
OKAY, OKAY. I'M HERE. I WON'T LEAVE YOU.
I WON'T LEAVE YOU...

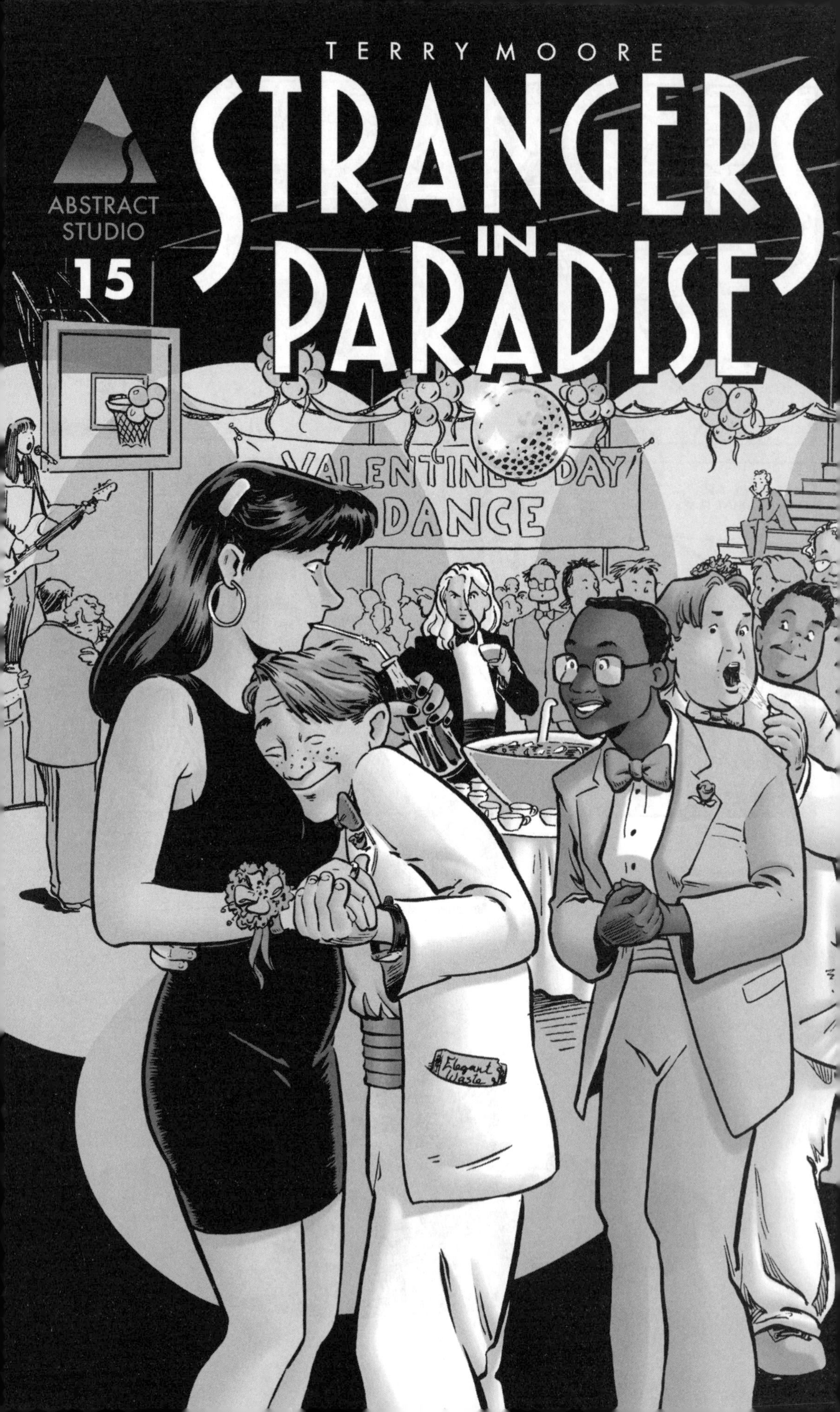
TERRY MOORE
STRANGERS IN PARADISE
ABSTRACT STUDIO
15
VALENTINE'S DAY DANCE
Elegant Waste

The Cowboy

There's a man drinking across the room.
He's been giving me glances of doom.
I've been watching him in between hands.
I'm gonna wait till he tips off his plans.

There's a numbness in me that's so cold.
It's a feeling that I've had before.
One by one all the sounds fade away.
And all my senses are flooded with hate.

I feel the passion in me burn my face.
Wipe the sweat off my hands on my lace.
There's a deafening ring in my head.
I try to picture the face I see dead.
I watch the man as he stands from his chair.
Never once does he let down his stare.
It's a showdown, we stand face to face.
Without warning his draw starts the race.

There's a numbness in me that's so cold.
It's a feeling that I've had before.
One by one all the sounds fade away,
And all my senses are flooded with hate.

People turn back to finish their drinks,
They know the cowboy is only a jinx.
And I stare in a trance at my fear,
At the cracks of six holes in a mirror.
As the numbness in me fades away,
I hope the feeling is gone for today.
I look at the floor and kneel down,
Pick a piece of my face off the ground.

There's a numbness in me that's so cold.
It's a feeling that I've had before.
One by one all the sounds fade away,
And all my senses are flooded with hate.

by Griffin Silver
from *Elegant Waste*

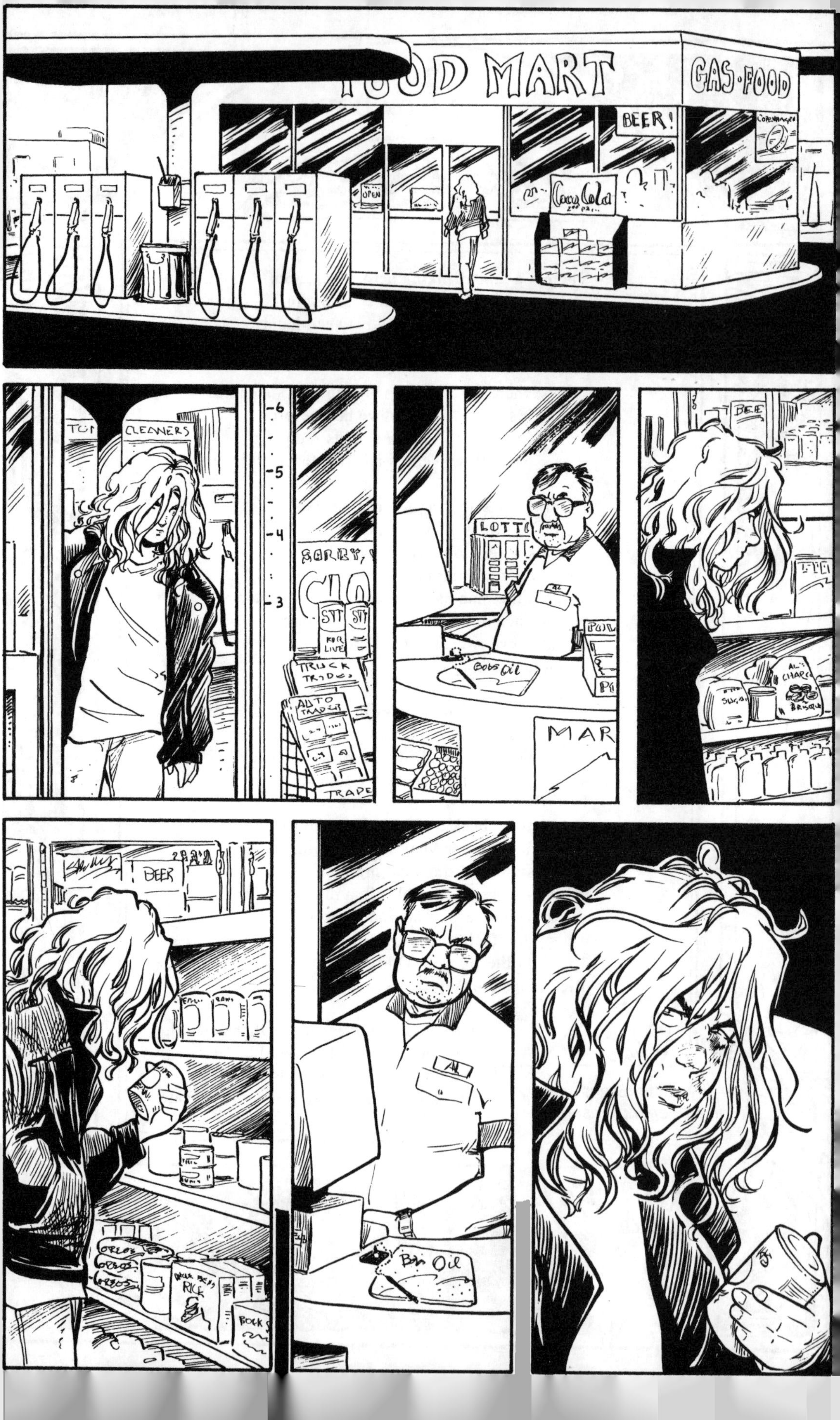
FOOD MART
GAS·FOOD
BEER!
OPEN
CLEANERS
TRUCK
AUTO TRADER
Bob's Oil
DEER
RICE
Bob's Oil

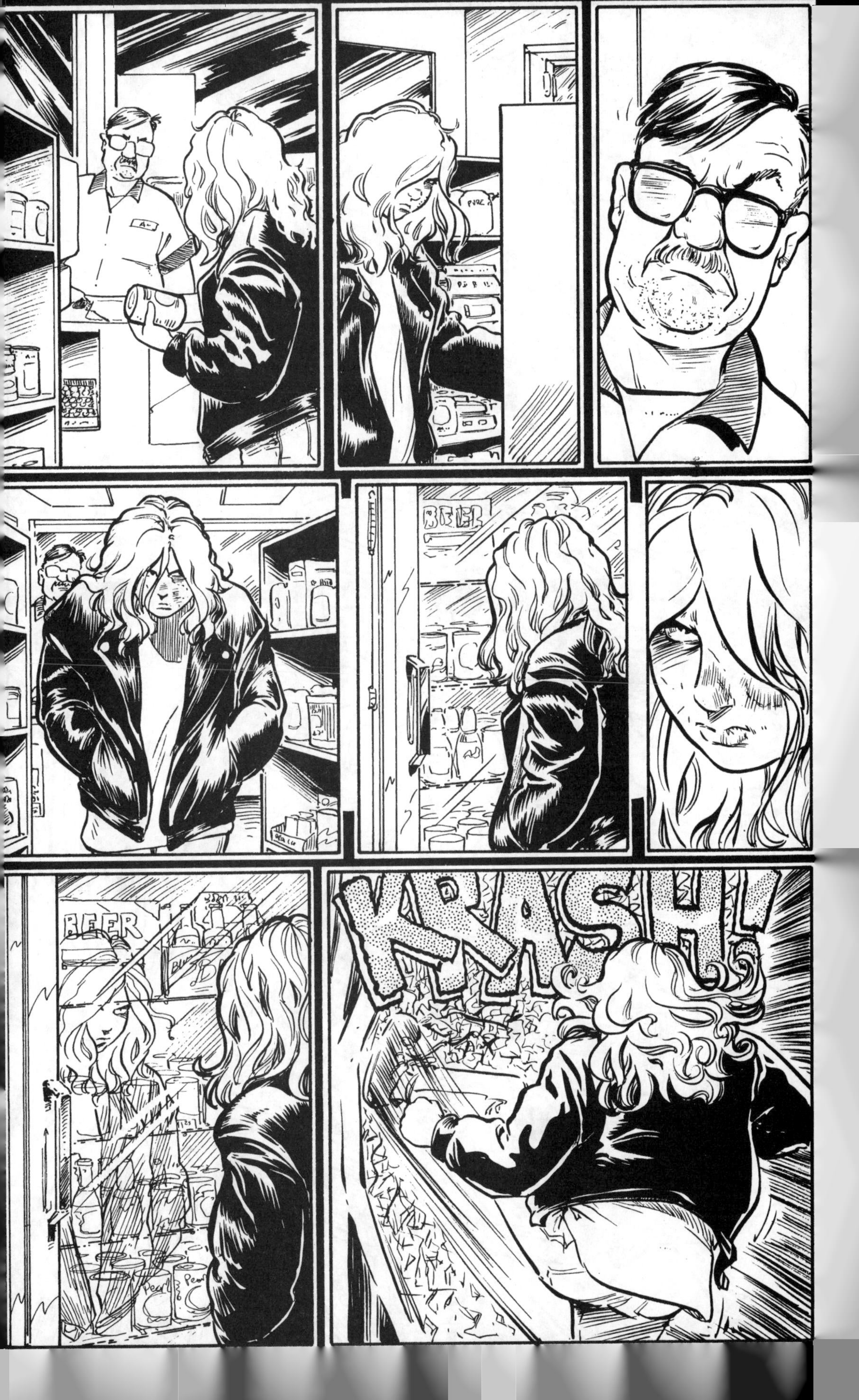
BEER
KRASH!

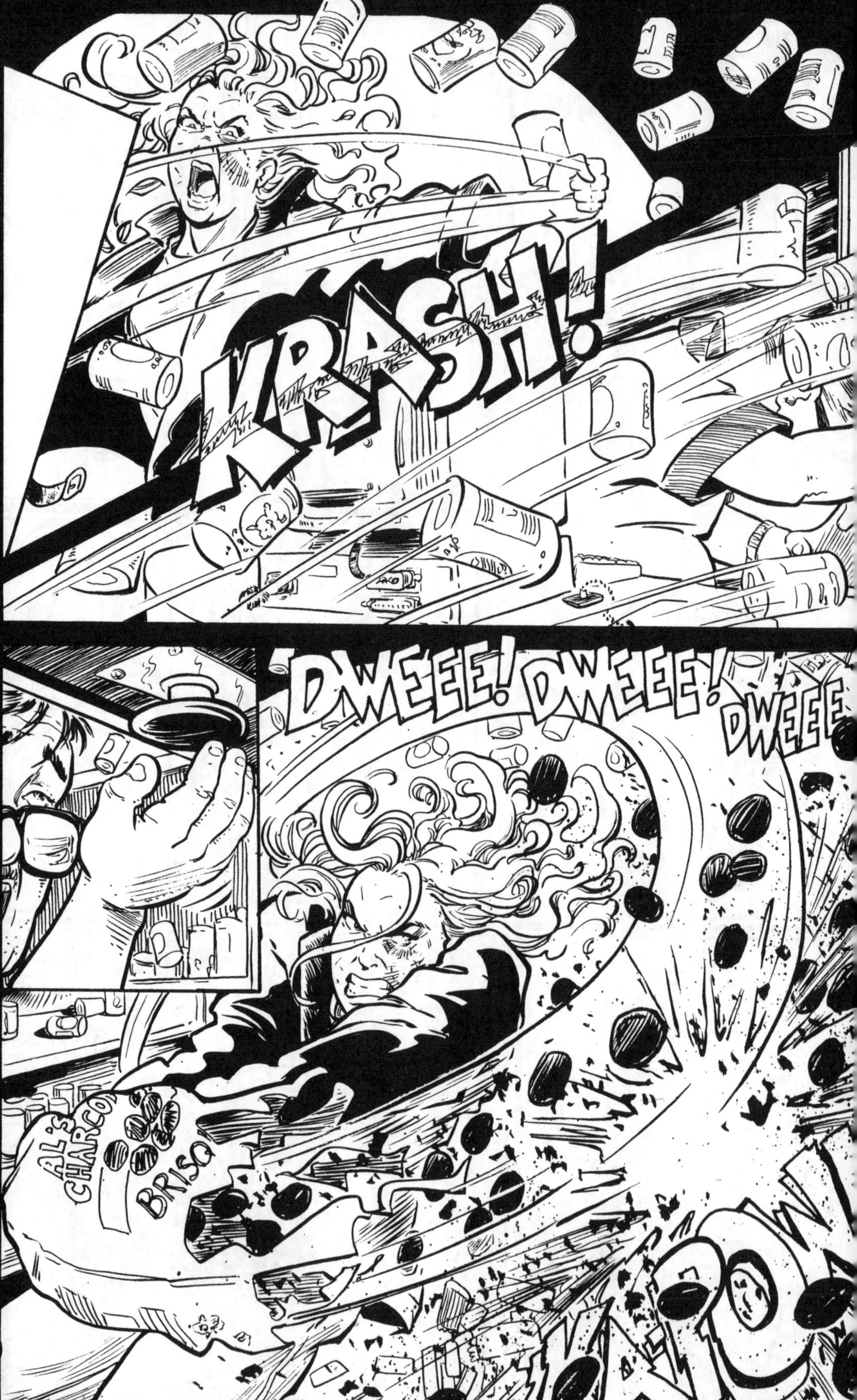
KRASH!
DWEEE! DWEEE!
DWEEE

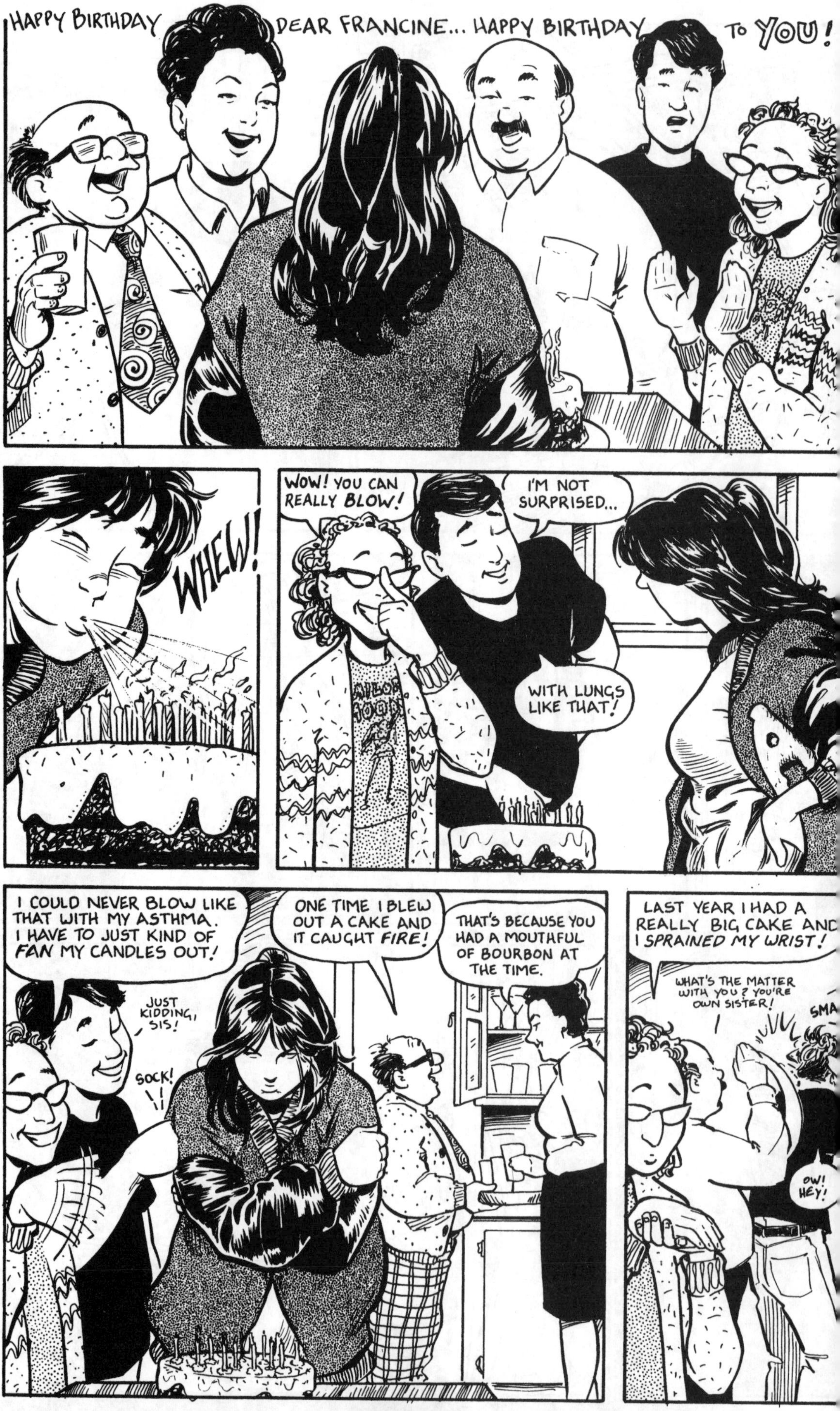

HAPPY BIRTHDAY
DEAR FRANCINE... HAPPY BIRTHDAY
TO YOU!
WHEW!
WOW! YOU CAN REALLY BLOW!
I'M NOT SURPRISED...
WITH LUNGS LIKE THAT!
I COULD NEVER BLOW LIKE THAT WITH MY ASTHMA. I HAVE TO JUST KIND OF FAN MY CANDLES OUT!
JUST KIDDING, SIS!
SOCK!
ONE TIME I BLEW OUT A CAKE AND IT CAUGHT FIRE!
THAT'S BECAUSE YOU HAD A MOUTHFUL OF BOURBON AT THE TIME.
LAST YEAR I HAD A REALLY BIG CAKE AND I SPRAINED MY WRIST!
WHAT'S THE MATTER WITH YOU? YOU'RE OWN SISTER!
OW! HEY!

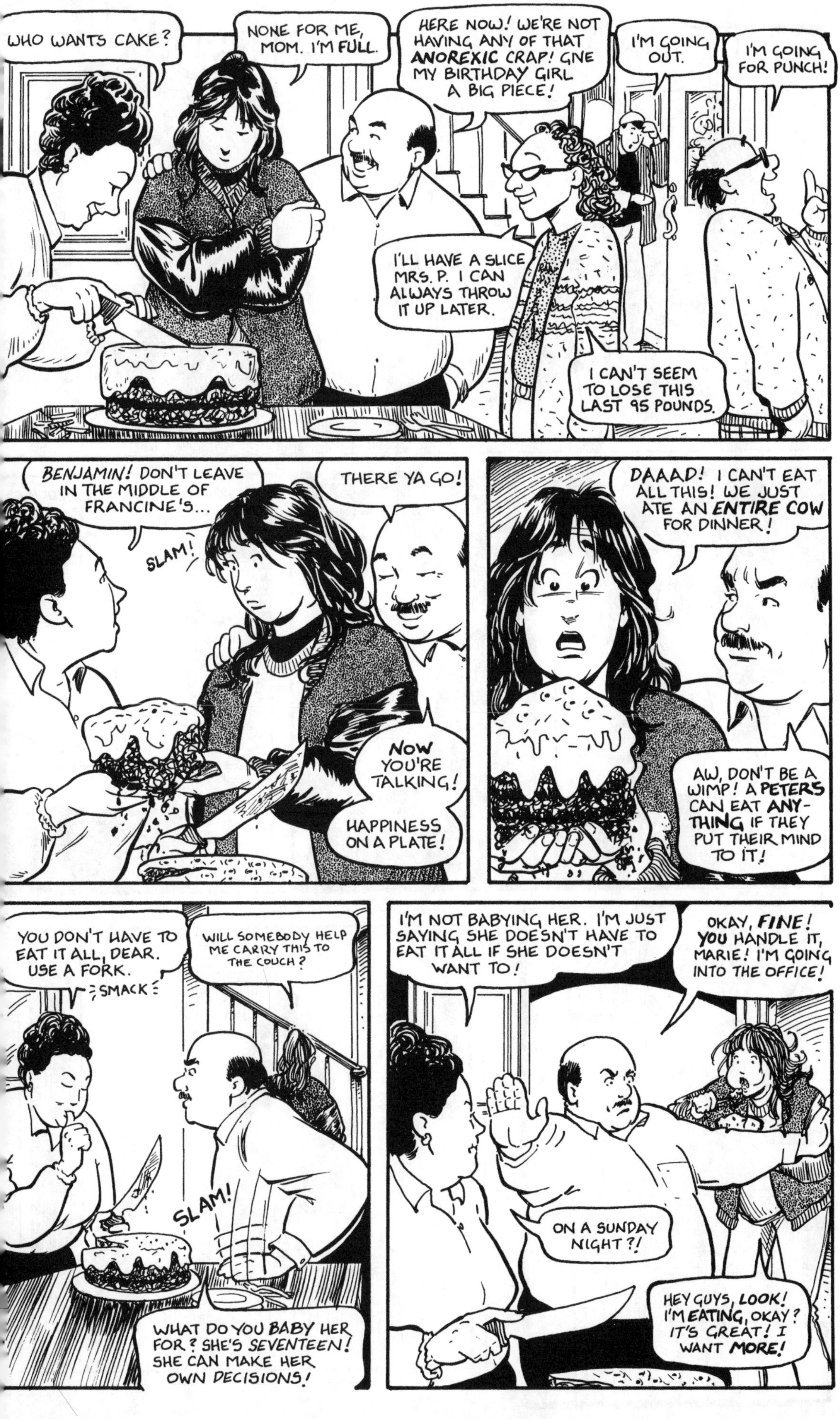
WHO WANTS CAKE?
NONE FOR ME, MOM. I'M FULL.
HERE NOW! WE'RE NOT HAVING ANY OF THAT ANOREXIC CRAP! GIVE MY BIRTHDAY GIRL A BIG PIECE!
I'M GOING OUT.
I'M GOING FOR PUNCH!
I'LL HAVE A SLICE MRS. P. I CAN ALWAYS THROW IT UP LATER.
I CAN'T SEEM TO LOSE THIS LAST 95 POUNDS.
BENJAMIN! DON'T LEAVE IN THE MIDDLE OF FRANCINE'S...
SLAM!
THERE YA GO!
NOW YOU'RE TALKING!
HAPPINESS ON A PLATE!
DAAAD! I CAN'T EAT ALL THIS! WE JUST ATE AN ENTIRE COW FOR DINNER!
AW, DON'T BE A WIMP! A PETERS CAN EAT ANYTHING IF THEY PUT THEIR MIND TO IT!
YOU DON'T HAVE TO EAT IT ALL, DEAR. USE A FORK.
SMACK
WILL SOMEBODY HELP ME CARRY THIS TO THE COUCH?
SLAM!
WHAT DO YOU BABY HER FOR? SHE'S SEVENTEEN! SHE CAN MAKE HER OWN DECISIONS!
I'M NOT BABYING HER. I'M JUST SAYING SHE DOESN'T HAVE TO EAT IT ALL IF SHE DOESN'T WANT TO!
OKAY, FINE! YOU HANDLE IT, MARIE! I'M GOING INTO THE OFFICE!
ON A SUNDAY NIGHT?!
HEY GUYS, LOOK! I'M EATING, OKAY? IT'S GREAT! I WANT MORE!

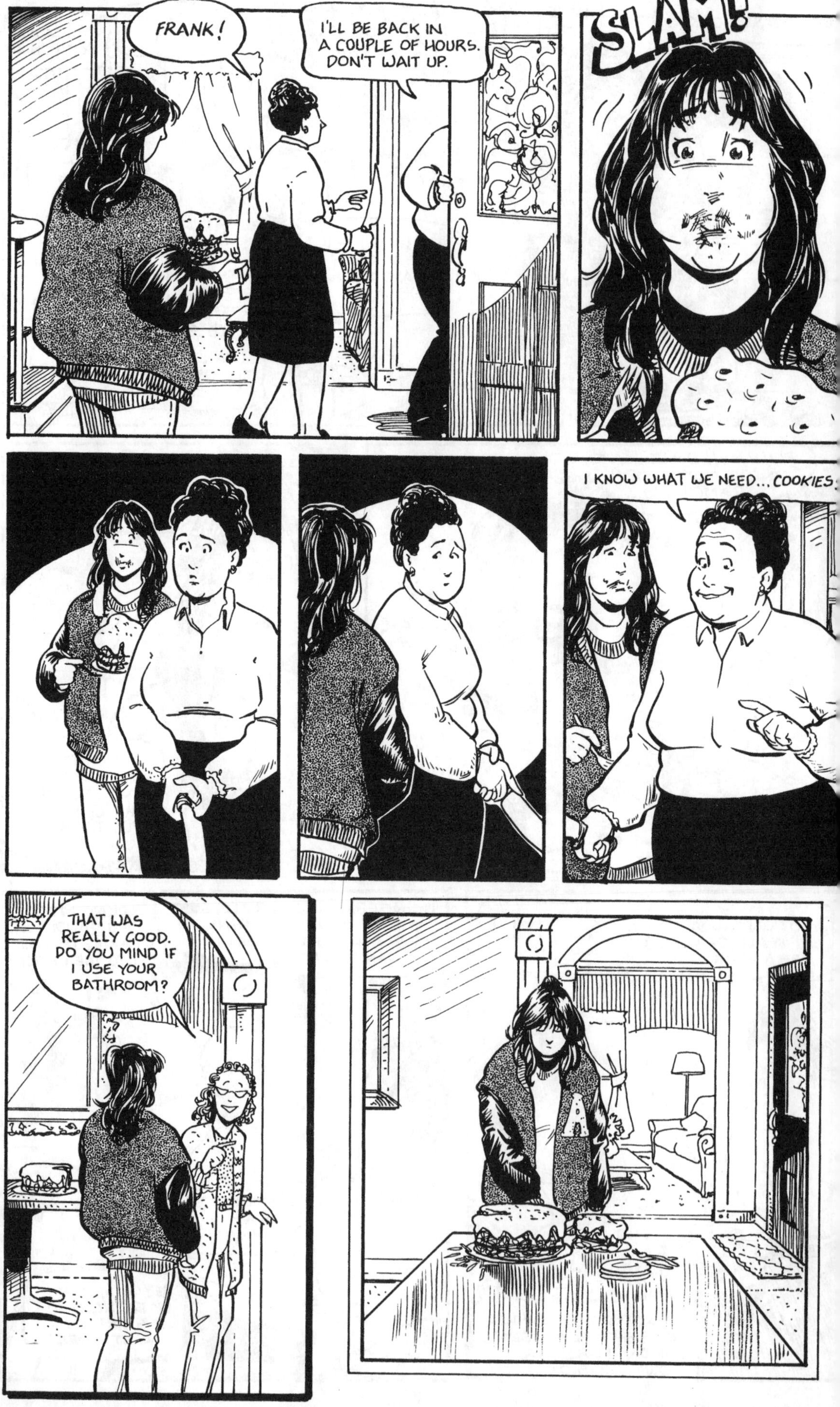
FRANK!
I'LL BE BACK IN A COUPLE OF HOURS. DON'T WAIT UP.
SLAM!
I KNOW WHAT WE NEED... COOKIES
THAT WAS REALLY GOOD. DO YOU MIND IF I USE YOUR BATHROOM?

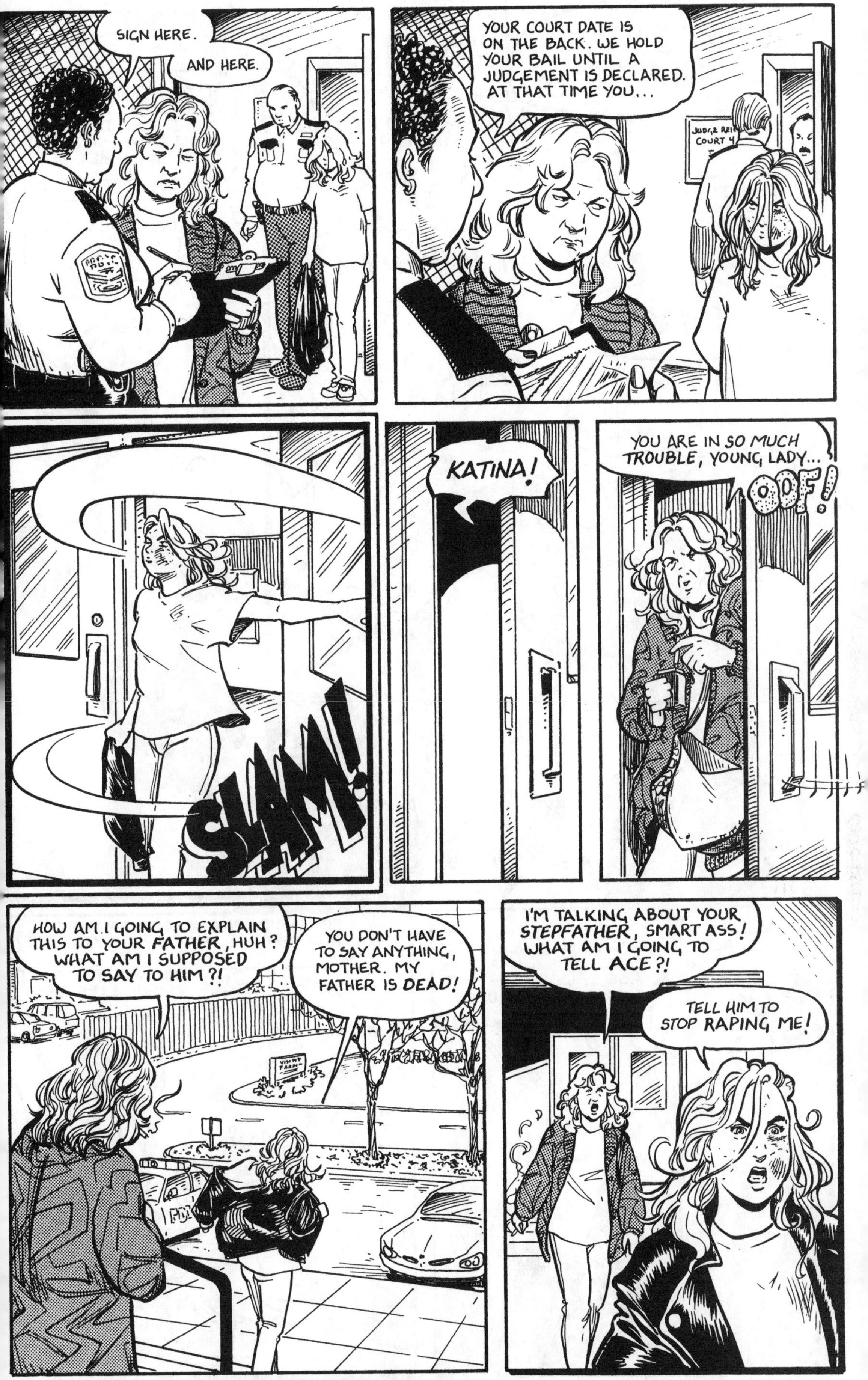
SIGN HERE.
AND HERE.
YOUR COURT DATE IS ON THE BACK. WE HOLD YOUR BAIL UNTIL A JUDGEMENT IS DECLARED. AT THAT TIME YOU...
COURT 4
SLAM!
KATINA!
YOU ARE IN SO MUCH TROUBLE, YOUNG LADY...
OOF!
HOW AM I GOING TO EXPLAIN THIS TO YOUR FATHER, HUH? WHAT AM I SUPPOSED TO SAY TO HIM ?!
YOU DON'T HAVE TO SAY ANYTHING, MOTHER. MY FATHER IS DEAD!
I'M TALKING ABOUT YOUR STEPFATHER, SMART ASS! WHAT AM I GOING TO TELL ACE ?!
TELL HIM TO STOP RAPING ME!

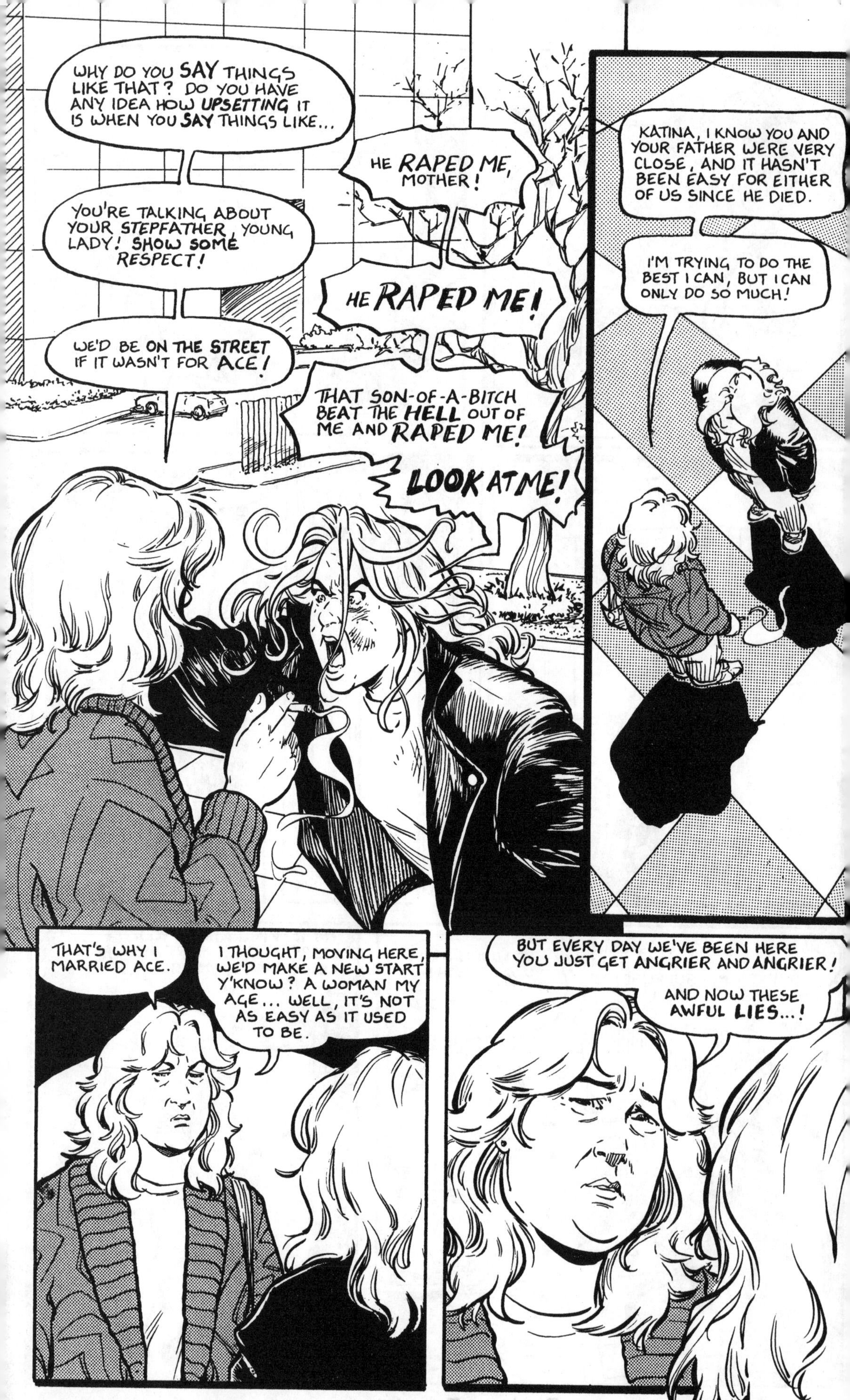
WHY DO YOU SAY THINGS LIKE THAT? DO YOU HAVE ANY IDEA HOW UPSETTING IT IS WHEN YOU SAY THINGS LIKE...
HE RAPED ME, MOTHER!
YOU'RE TALKING ABOUT YOUR STEPFATHER, YOUNG LADY! SHOW SOME RESPECT!
HE RAPED ME!
WE'D BE ON THE STREET IF IT WASN'T FOR ACE!
THAT SON-OF-A-BITCH BEAT THE HELL OUT OF ME AND RAPED ME!
LOOK AT ME!
KATINA, I KNOW YOU AND YOUR FATHER WERE VERY CLOSE, AND IT HASN'T BEEN EASY FOR EITHER OF US SINCE HE DIED.
I'M TRYING TO DO THE BEST I CAN, BUT I CAN ONLY DO SO MUCH!
THAT'S WHY I MARRIED ACE.
I THOUGHT, MOVING HERE, WE'D MAKE A NEW START Y'KNOW? A WOMAN MY AGE... WELL, IT'S NOT AS EASY AS IT USED TO BE.
BUT EVERY DAY WE'VE BEEN HERE YOU JUST GET ANGRIER AND ANGRIER!
AND NOW THESE AWFUL LIES...!

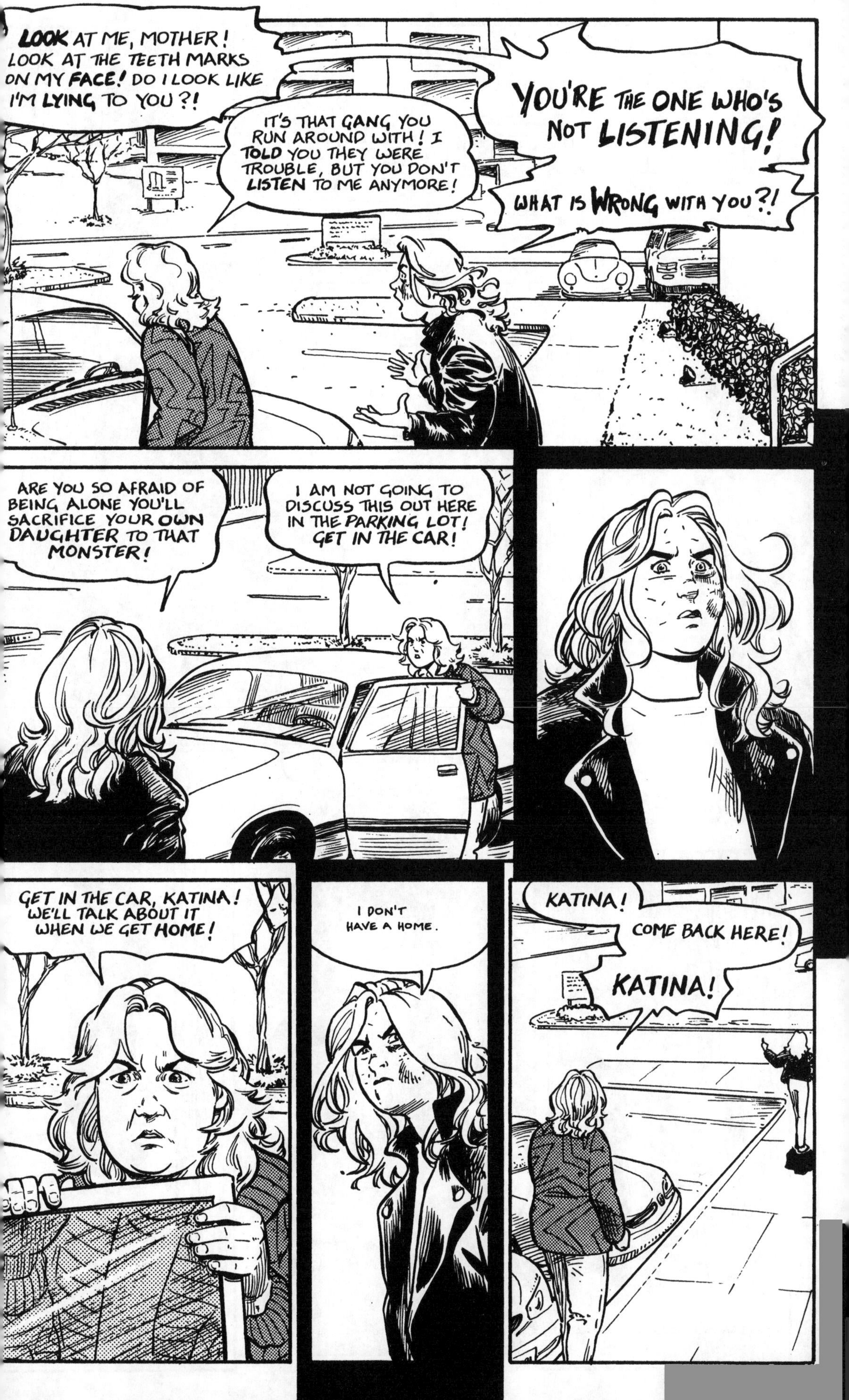
LOOK AT ME, MOTHER! LOOK AT THE TEETH MARKS ON MY FACE! DO I LOOK LIKE I'M LYING TO YOU?!
IT'S THAT GANG YOU RUN AROUND WITH! I TOLD YOU THEY WERE TROUBLE, BUT YOU DON'T LISTEN TO ME ANYMORE!
YOU'RE THE ONE WHO'S NOT LISTENING!
WHAT IS WRONG WITH YOU?!
ARE YOU SO AFRAID OF BEING ALONE YOU'LL SACRIFICE YOUR OWN DAUGHTER TO THAT MONSTER!
I AM NOT GOING TO DISCUSS THIS OUT HERE IN THE PARKING LOT! GET IN THE CAR!
GET IN THE CAR, KATINA! WE'LL TALK ABOUT IT WHEN WE GET HOME!
I DON'T HAVE A HOME.
KATINA!
COME BACK HERE!
KATINA!

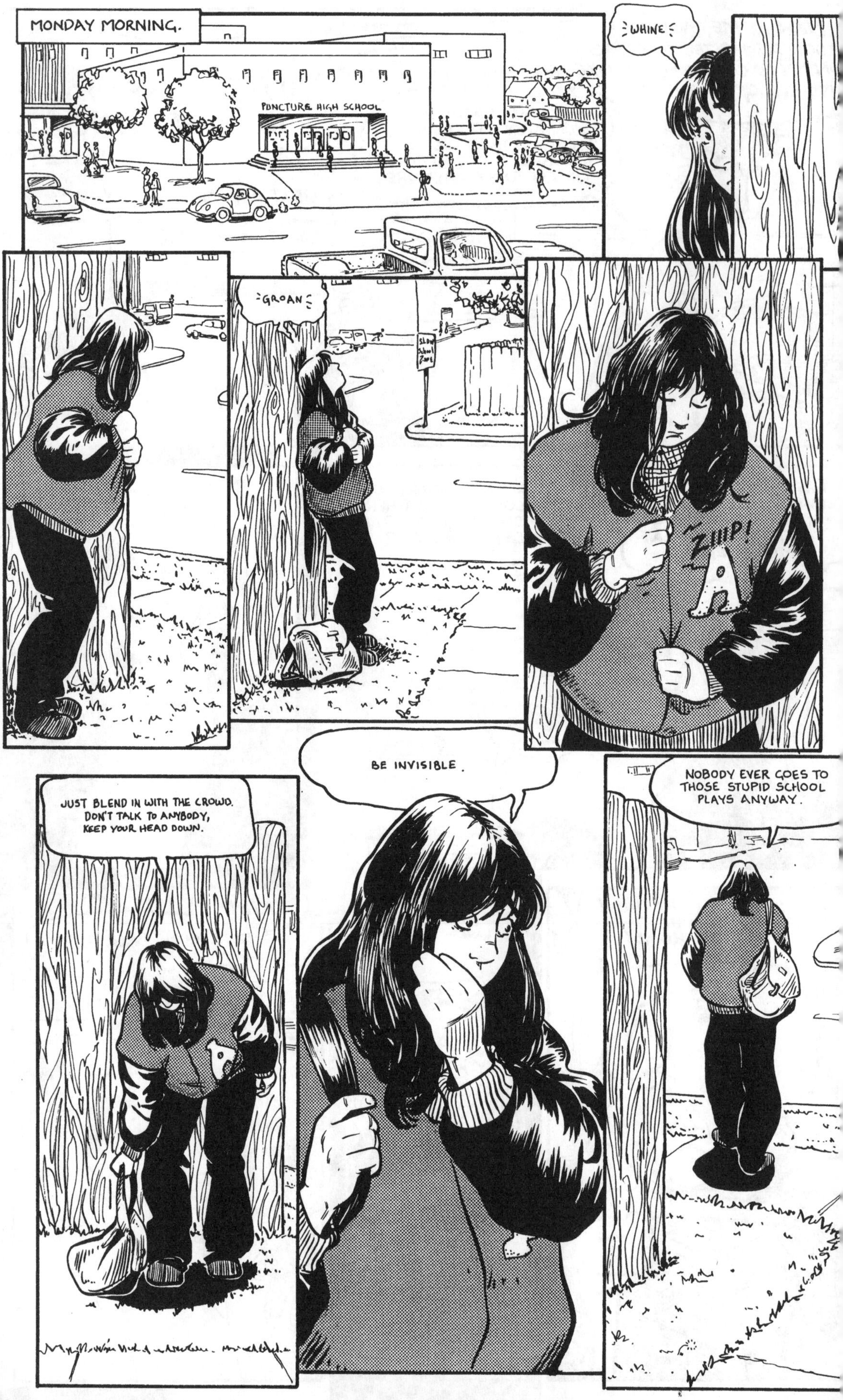
MONDAY MORNING.
PUNCTURE HIGH SCHOOL
WHINE
GROAN
SLOW School Zone
ZIIIP!
JUST BLEND IN WITH THE CROWD. DON'T TALK TO ANYBODY, KEEP YOUR HEAD DOWN.
BE INVISIBLE.
NOBODY EVER GOES TO THOSE STUPID SCHOOL PLAYS ANYWAY.

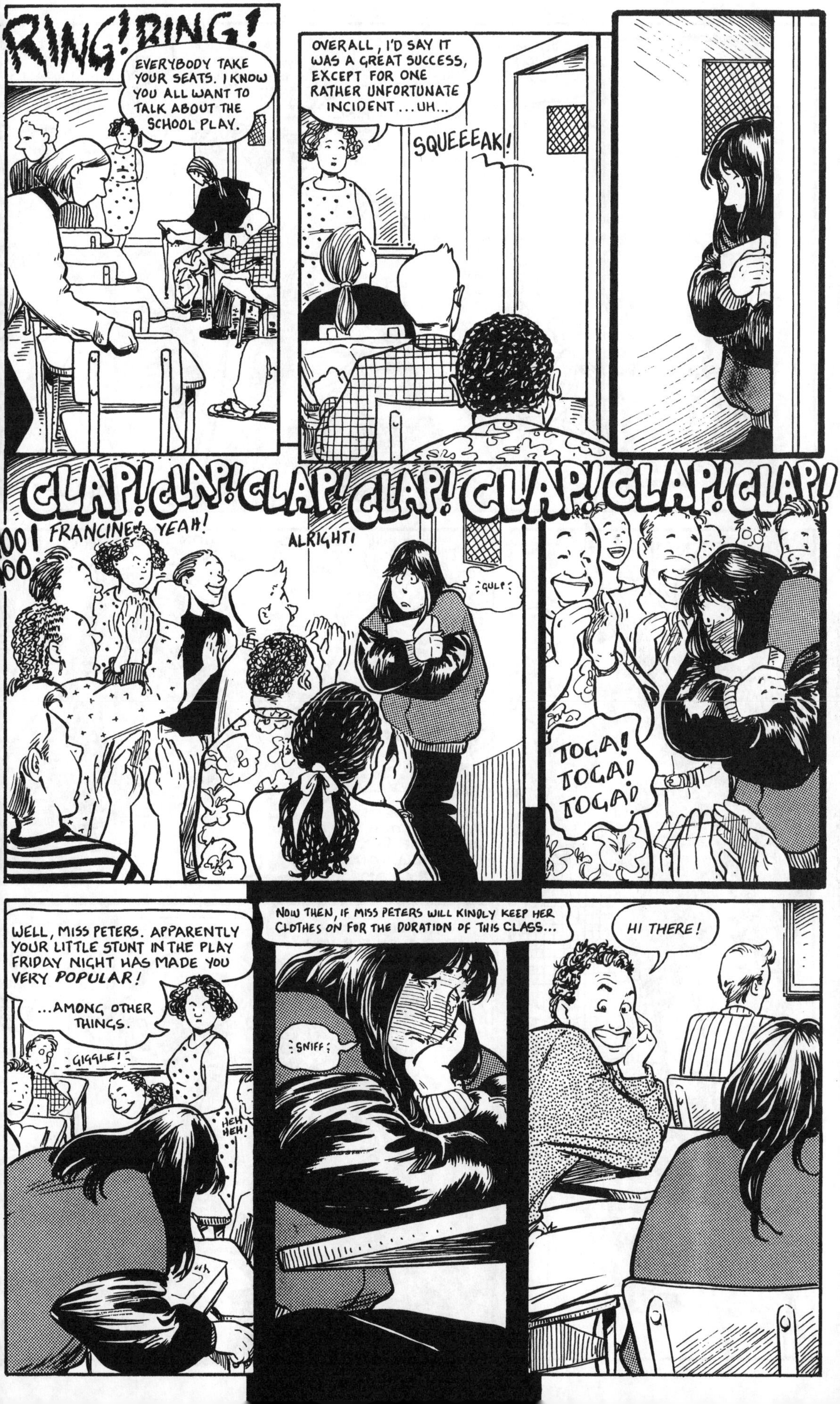
RING! RING!
EVERYBODY TAKE YOUR SEATS. I KNOW YOU ALL WANT TO TALK ABOUT THE SCHOOL PLAY.
OVERALL, I'D SAY IT WAS A GREAT SUCCESS, EXCEPT FOR ONE RATHER UNFORTUNATE INCIDENT... UH...
SQUEEEAK!
CLAP! CLAP! CLAP! CLAP! CLAP! CLAP! CLAP!
FRANCINE! YEAH!
ALRIGHT!
GULP
TOGA! TOGA! TOGA!
WELL, MISS PETERS. APPARENTLY YOUR LITTLE STUNT IN THE PLAY FRIDAY NIGHT HAS MADE YOU VERY POPULAR!
...AMONG OTHER THINGS.
GIGGLE!
HEH HEH!
NOW THEN, IF MISS PETERS WILL KINDLY KEEP HER CLOTHES ON FOR THE DURATION OF THIS CLASS...
SNIFF
HI THERE!

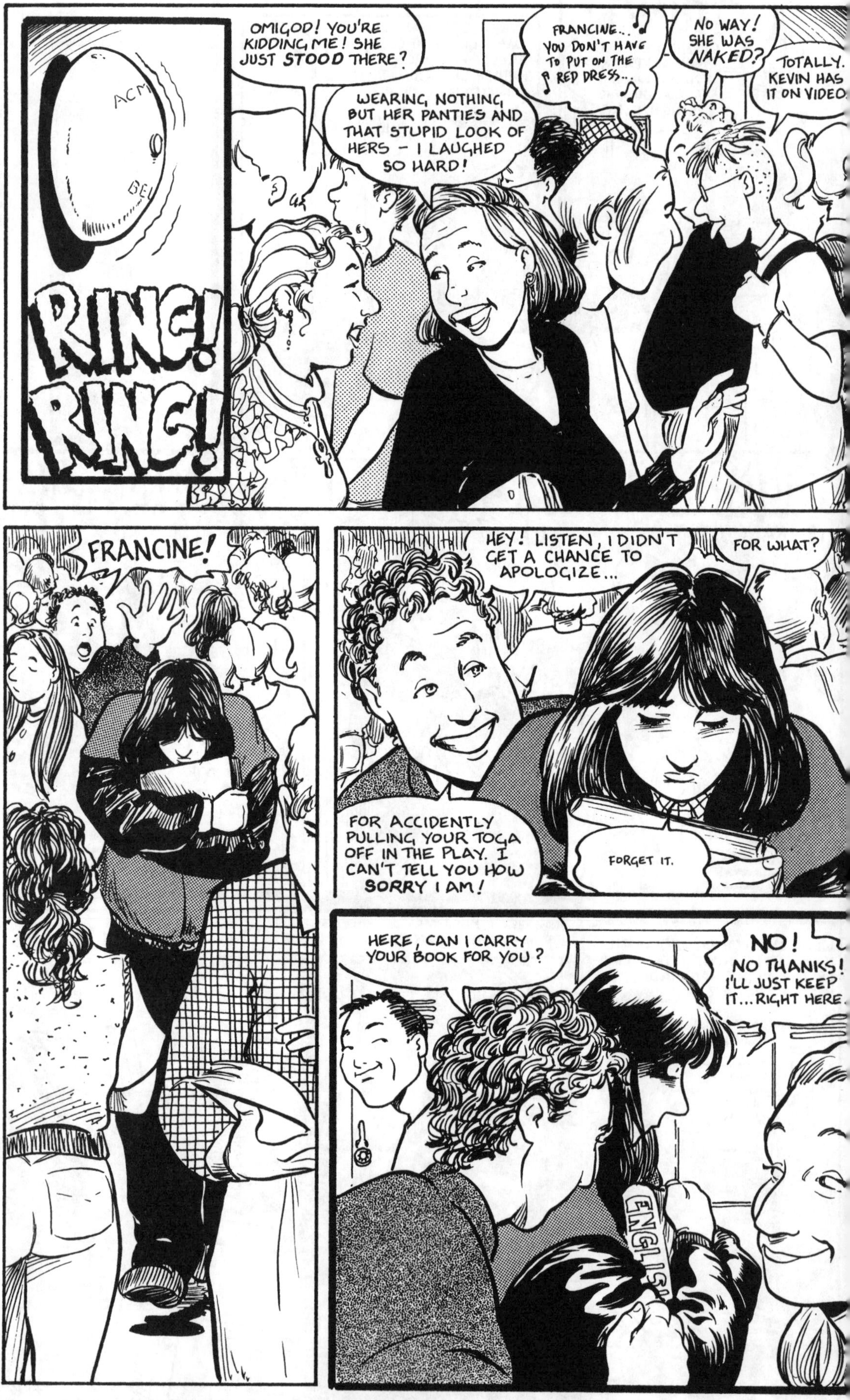
ACM
BEL
RING! RING!
OMIGOD! YOU'RE KIDDING ME! SHE JUST STOOD THERE?
WEARING NOTHING BUT HER PANTIES AND THAT STUPID LOOK OF HERS - I LAUGHED SO HARD!
FRANCINE.. YOU DON'T HAVE TO PUT ON THE RED DRESS...
NO WAY! SHE WAS NAKED?
TOTALLY. KEVIN HAS IT ON VIDEO
FRANCINE!
HEY! LISTEN, I DIDN'T GET A CHANCE TO APOLOGIZE...
FOR WHAT?
FOR ACCIDENTLY PULLING YOUR TOGA OFF IN THE PLAY. I CAN'T TELL YOU HOW SORRY I AM!
FORGET IT.
HERE, CAN I CARRY YOUR BOOK FOR YOU?
NO! NO THANKS! I'LL JUST KEEP IT... RIGHT HERE.
ENGLISH

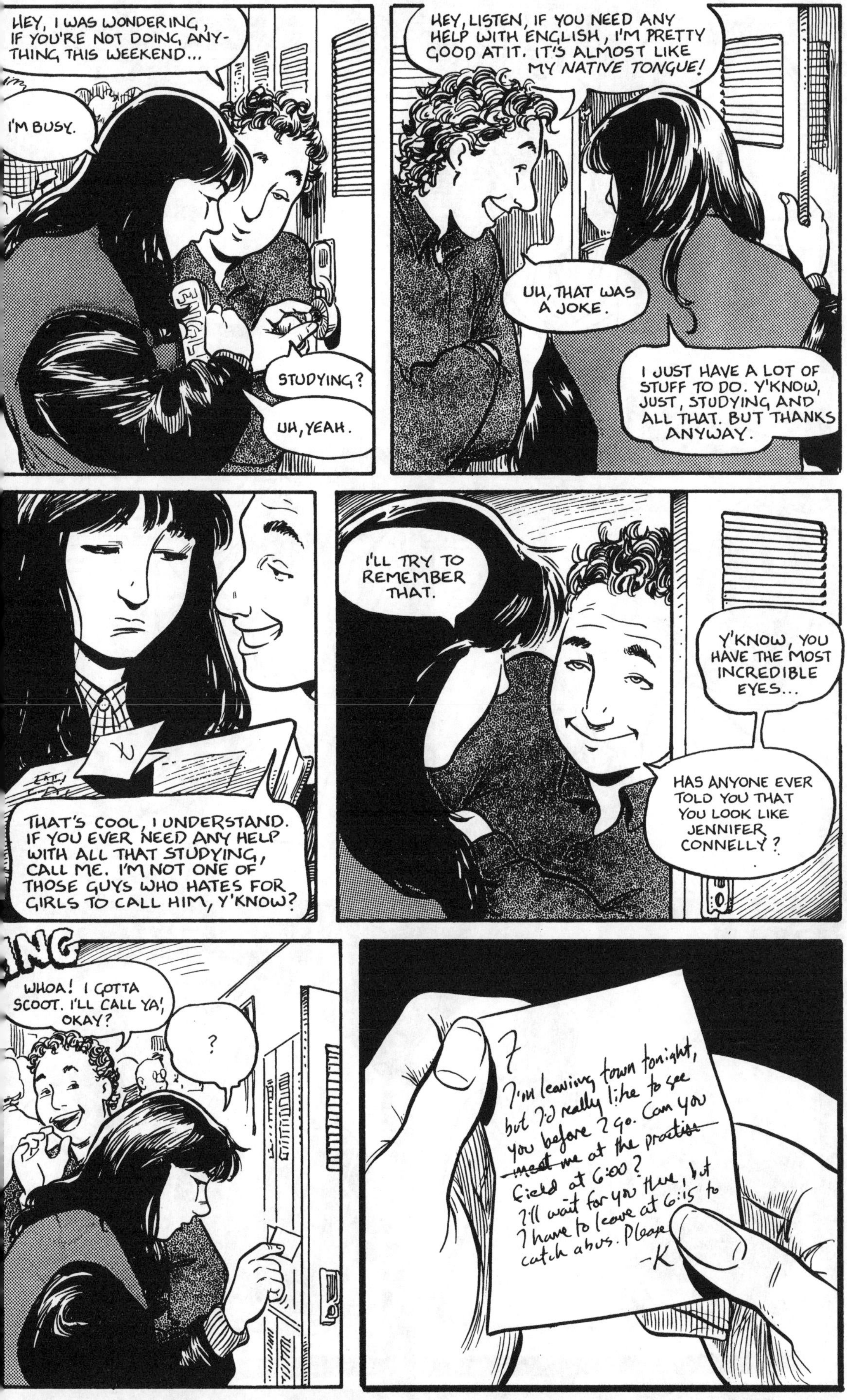
HEY, I WAS WONDERING, IF YOU'RE NOT DOING ANYTHING THIS WEEKEND...
I'M BUSY.
STUDYING?
UH, YEAH.
HEY, LISTEN, IF YOU NEED ANY HELP WITH ENGLISH, I'M PRETTY GOOD AT IT. IT'S ALMOST LIKE MY NATIVE TONGUE!
UH, THAT WAS A JOKE.
I JUST HAVE A LOT OF STUFF TO DO. Y'KNOW, JUST, STUDYING AND ALL THAT. BUT THANKS ANYWAY.
THAT'S COOL, I UNDERSTAND. IF YOU EVER NEED ANY HELP WITH ALL THAT STUDYING, CALL ME. I'M NOT ONE OF THOSE GUYS WHO HATES FOR GIRLS TO CALL HIM, Y'KNOW?
I'LL TRY TO REMEMBER THAT.
Y'KNOW, YOU HAVE THE MOST INCREDIBLE EYES...
HAS ANYONE EVER TOLD YOU THAT YOU LOOK LIKE JENNIFER CONNELLY?
ING
WHOA! I GOTTA SCOOT. I'LL CALL YA', OKAY?
?
I'm leaving town tonight, but I'd really like to see you before I go. Can you meet me at the practice field at 6:00? I'll wait for you there, but I have to leave at 6:15 to catch a bus. Please
-K

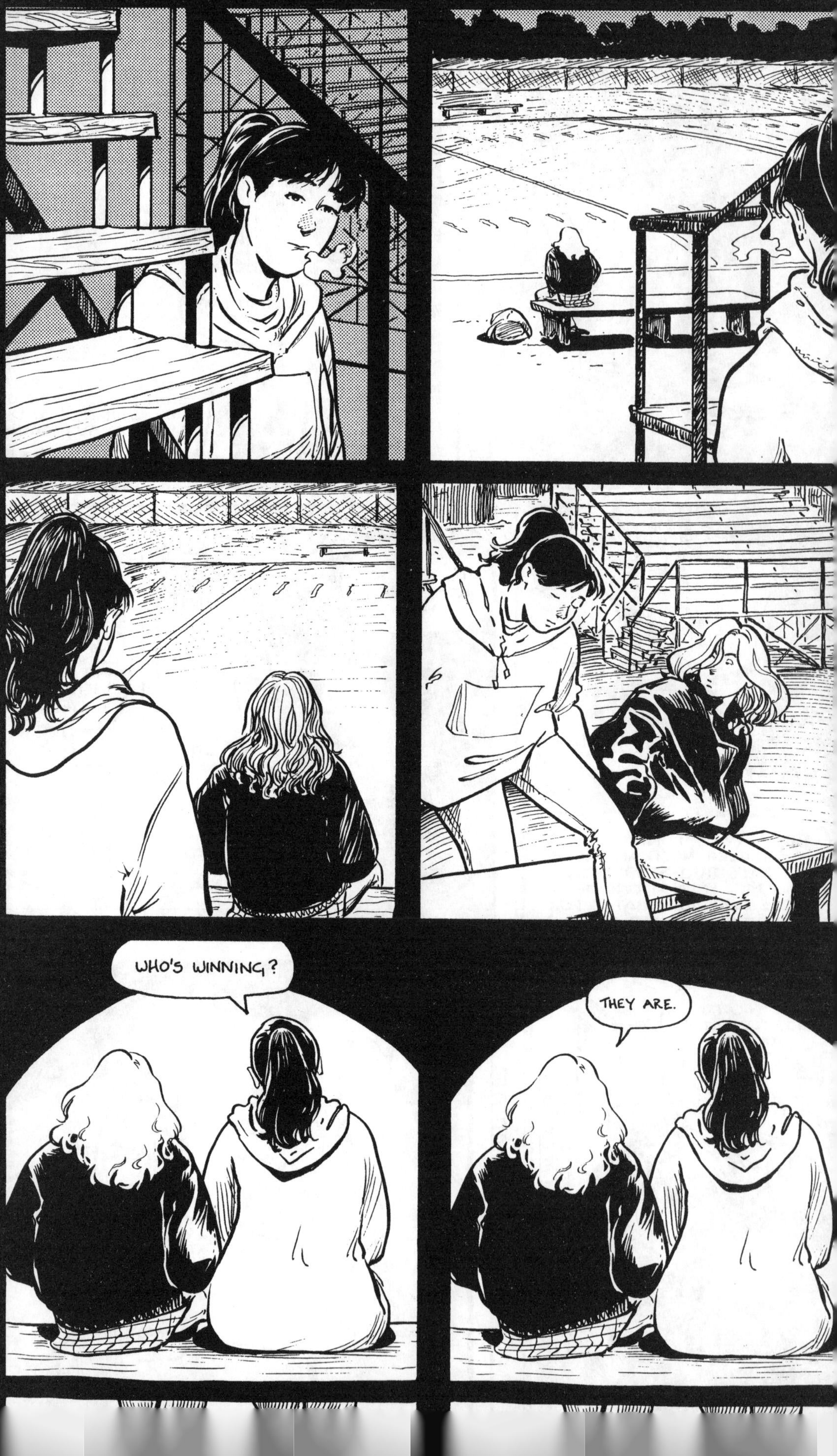
WHO'S WINNING?
THEY ARE.

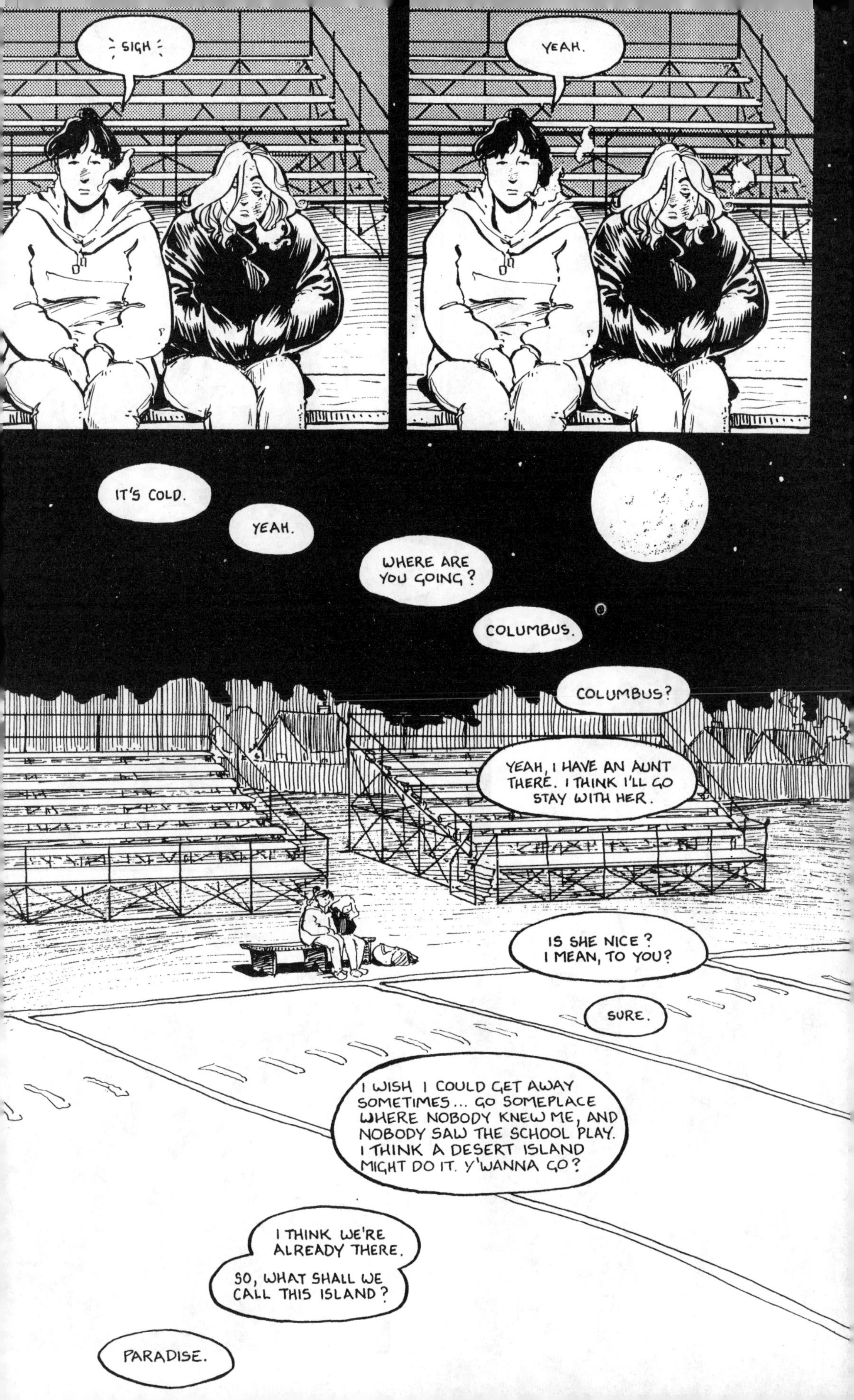
SIGH
YEAH.
IT'S COLD.
YEAH.
WHERE ARE YOU GOING?
COLUMBUS.
COLUMBUS?
YEAH, I HAVE AN AUNT THERE. I THINK I'LL GO STAY WITH HER.
IS SHE NICE? I MEAN, TO YOU?
SURE.
I WISH I COULD GET AWAY SOMETIMES... GO SOMEPLACE WHERE NOBODY KNEW ME, AND NOBODY SAW THE SCHOOL PLAY. I THINK A DESERT ISLAND MIGHT DO IT. Y'WANNA GO?
I THINK WE'RE ALREADY THERE.
SO, WHAT SHALL WE CALL THIS ISLAND?
PARADISE.

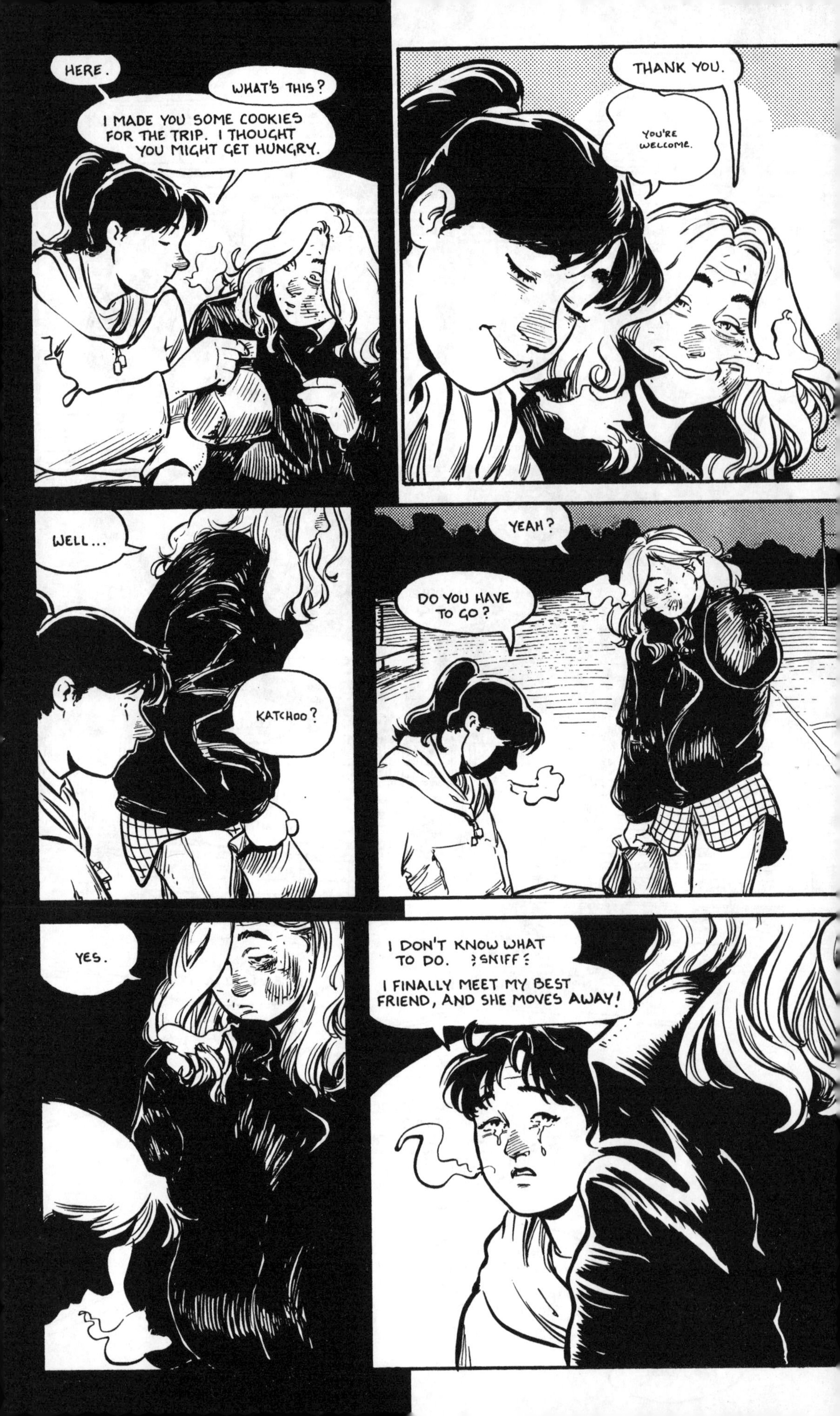
HERE.
WHAT'S THIS?
I MADE YOU SOME COOKIES FOR THE TRIP. I THOUGHT YOU MIGHT GET HUNGRY.
THANK YOU.
YOU'RE WELCOME.
WELL...
KATCHOO?
YEAH?
DO YOU HAVE TO GO?
YES.
I DON'T KNOW WHAT TO DO. SNIFF
I FINALLY MEET MY BEST FRIEND, AND SHE MOVES AWAY!

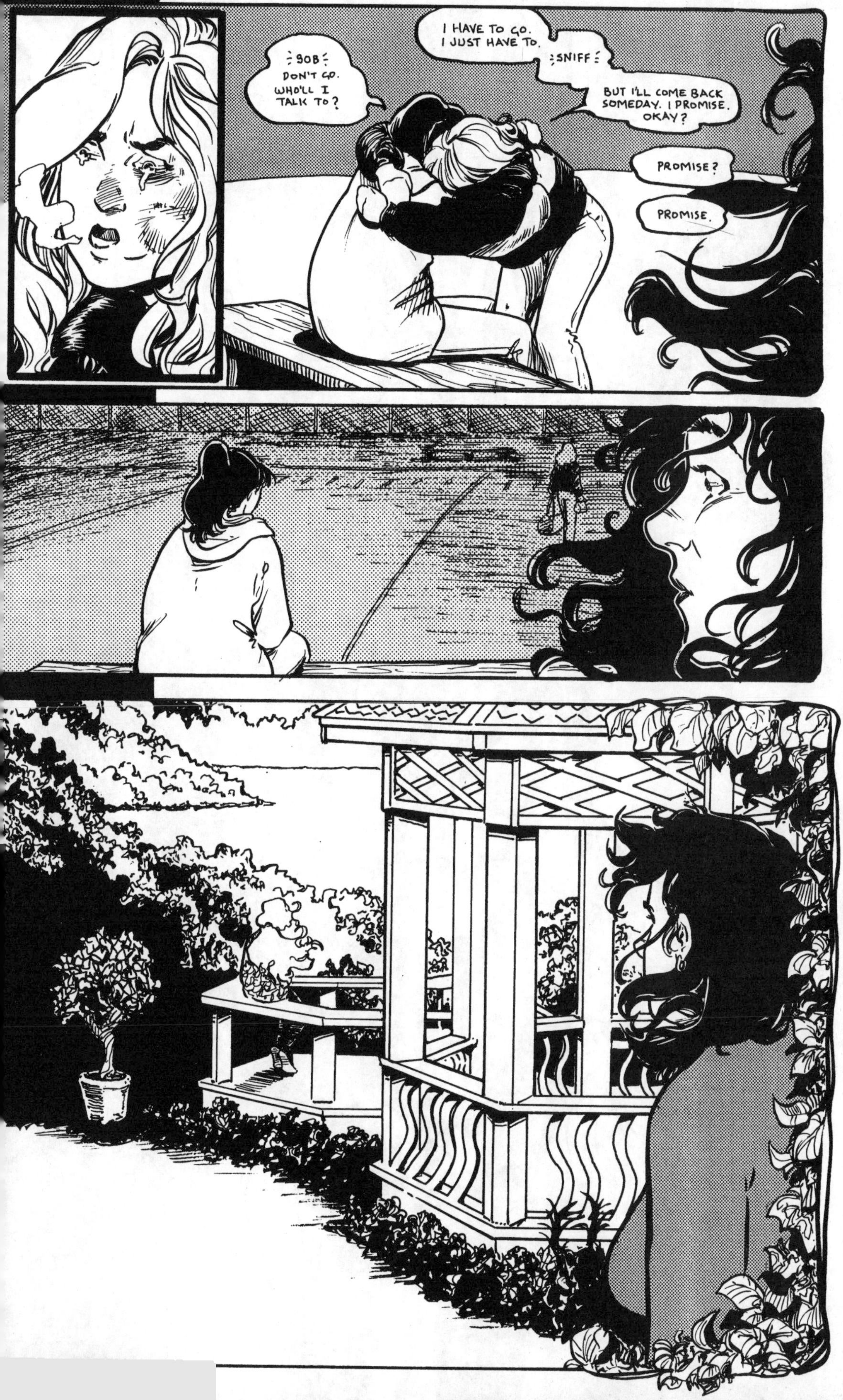

SOB
DON'T GO. WHO'LL I TALK TO?
I HAVE TO GO. I JUST HAVE TO.
SNIFF
BUT I'LL COME BACK SOMEDAY. I PROMISE. OKAY?
PROMISE?
PROMISE.

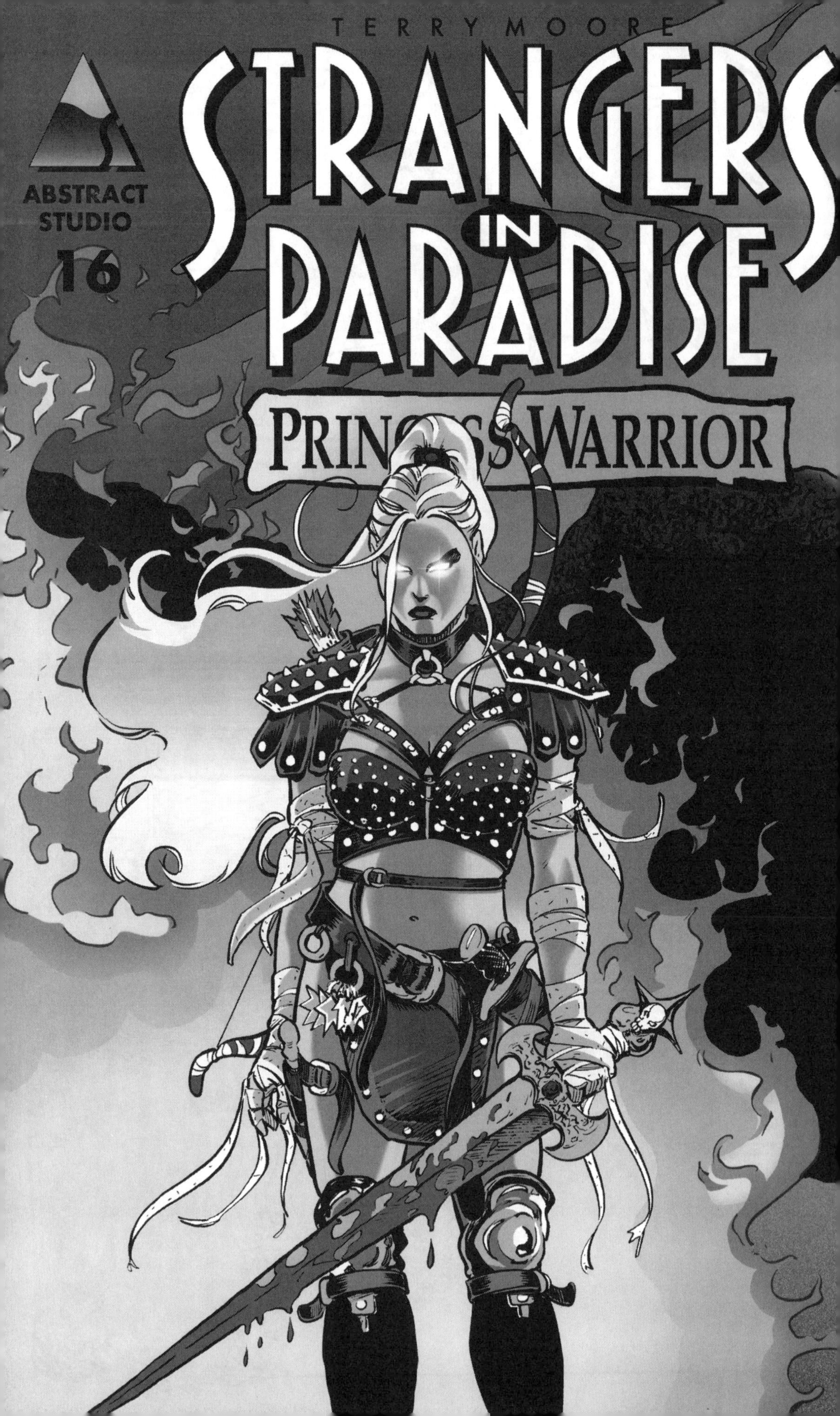

TERRY MOORE
STRANGERS IN PARADISE
ABSTRACT STUDIO
16
WARRIOR

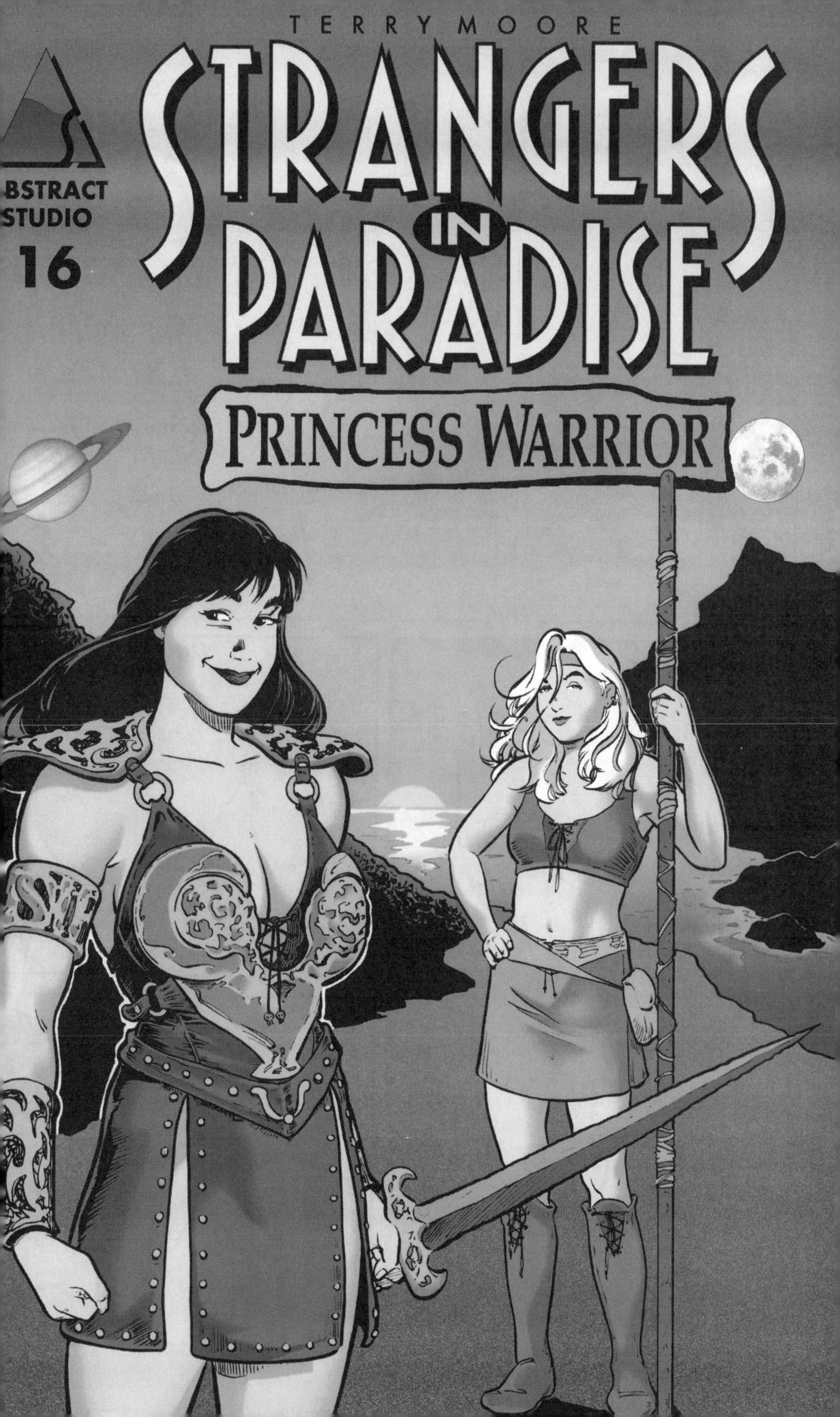
TERRY MOORE
STRANGERS IN PARADISE
BSTRACT
STUDIO
16
PRINCESS WARRIOR

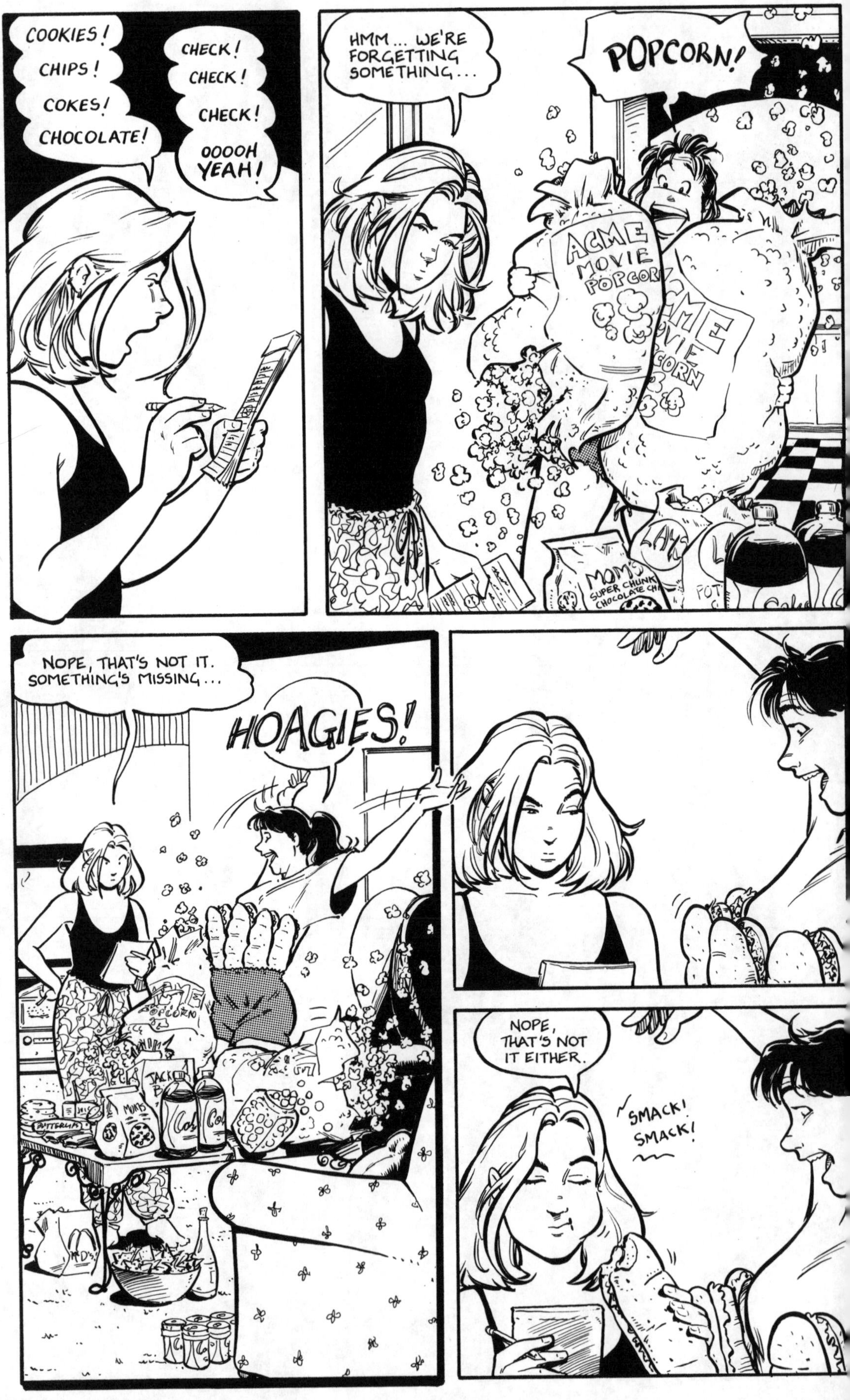
COOKIES!
CHIPS!
COKES!
CHOCOLATE!
CHECK!
CHECK!
CHECK!
OOOOH YEAH!
HMM... WE'RE FORGETTING SOMETHING...
POPCORN!
ACME MOVIE POPCORN
MOM'S SUPER CHUNK CHOCOLATE CH
NOPE, THAT'S NOT IT. SOMETHING'S MISSING...
HOAGIES!
NOPE, THAT'S NOT IT EITHER.
SMACK! SMACK!

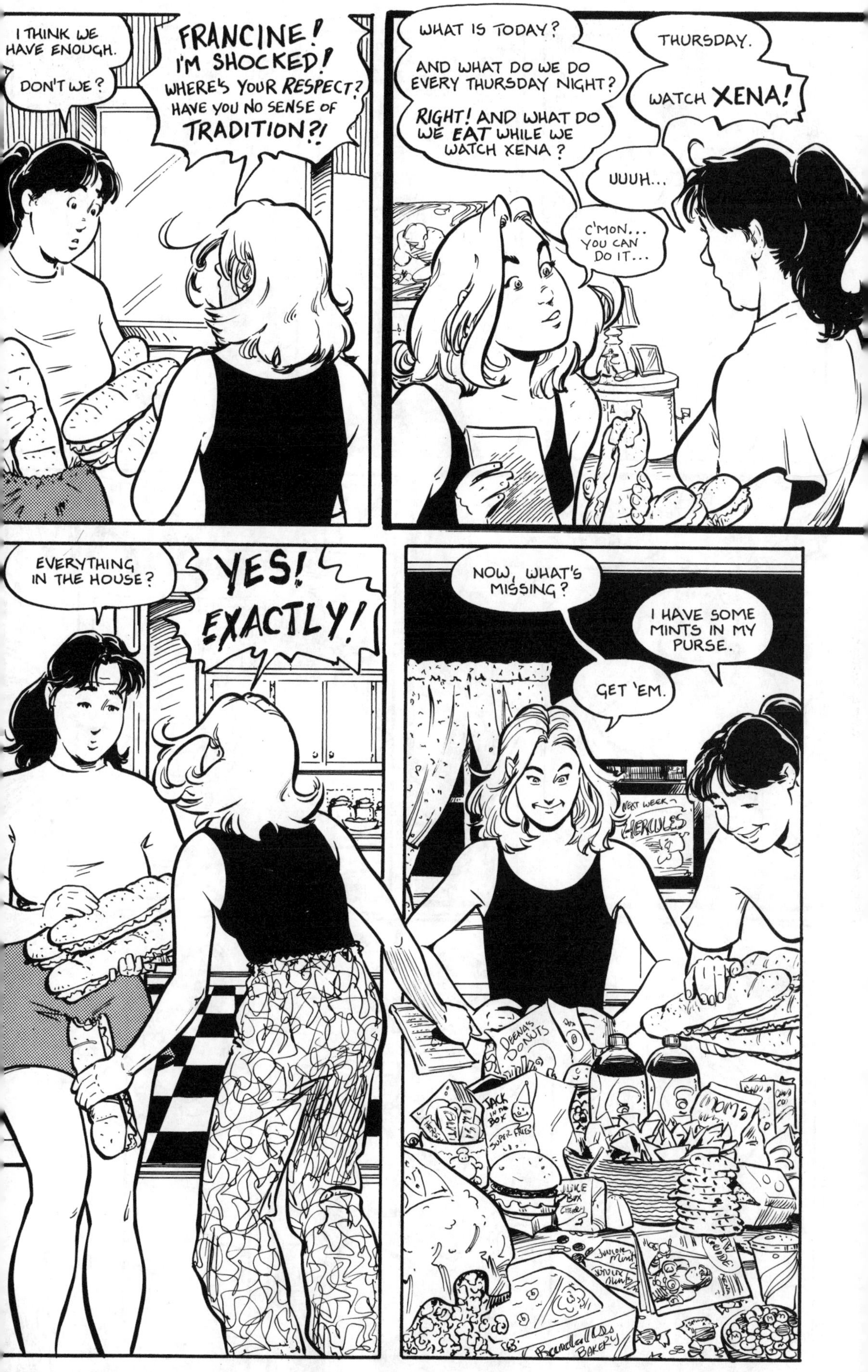

I THINK WE HAVE ENOUGH.
DON'T WE?
FRANCINE! I'M SHOCKED! WHERE'S YOUR RESPECT? HAVE YOU NO SENSE OF TRADITION?!
WHAT IS TODAY?
THURSDAY.
AND WHAT DO WE DO EVERY THURSDAY NIGHT?
WATCH XENA!
RIGHT! AND WHAT DO WE EAT WHILE WE WATCH XENA?
UUUH...
C'MON... YOU CAN DO IT...
EVERYTHING IN THE HOUSE?
YES! EXACTLY!
NOW, WHAT'S MISSING?
I HAVE SOME MINTS IN MY PURSE.
GET 'EM.
NEXT WEEK HERCULES
DEENA'S DONUTS
JACK IN THE BOX
SUPER FRIES
JUICE BOX
JUNIOR MINTS
BAKERY

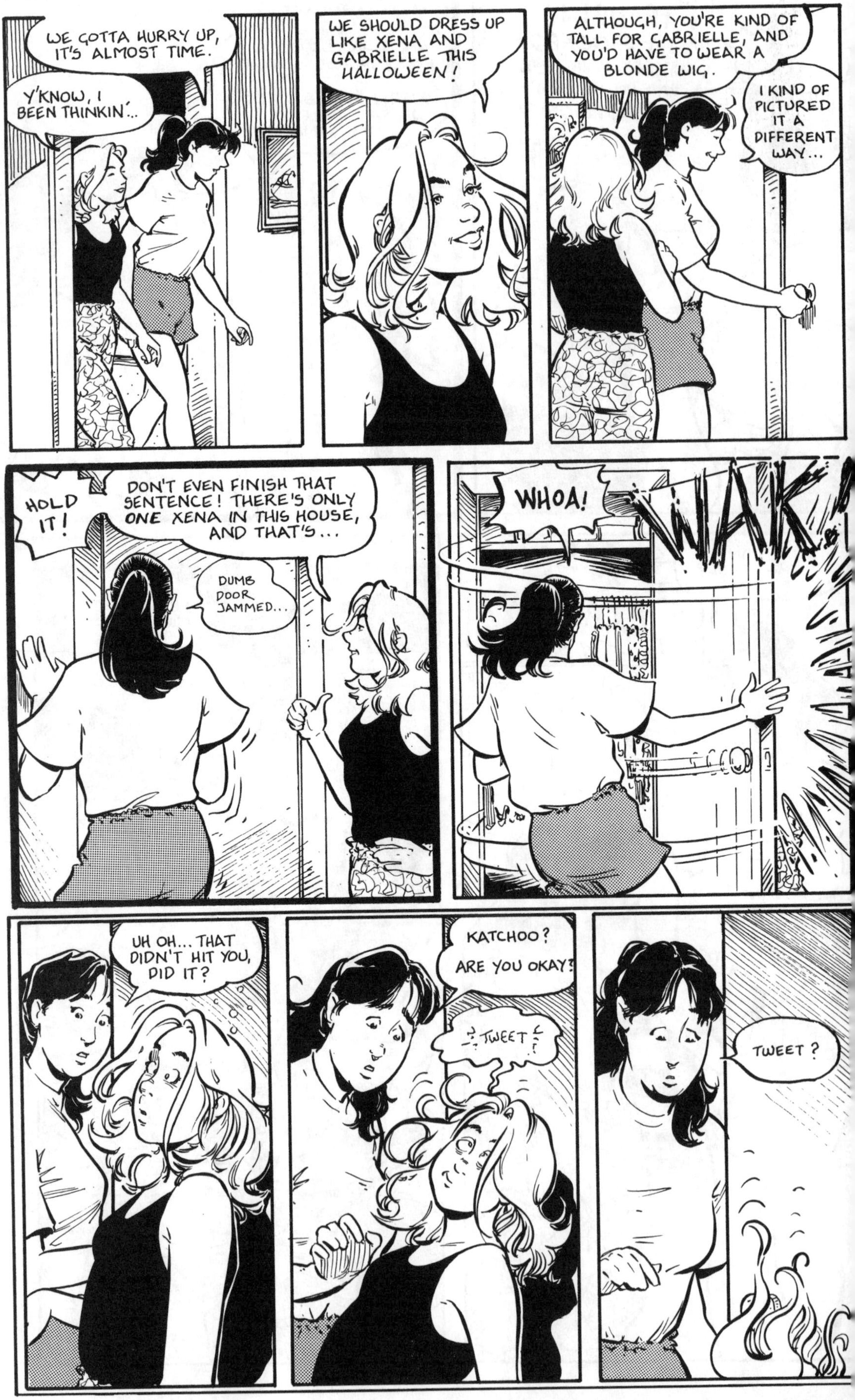
WE GOTTA HURRY UP, IT'S ALMOST TIME.
Y'KNOW, I BEEN THINKIN'...
WE SHOULD DRESS UP LIKE XENA AND GABRIELLE THIS HALLOWEEN!
ALTHOUGH, YOU'RE KIND OF TALL FOR GABRIELLE, AND YOU'D HAVE TO WEAR A BLONDE WIG.
I KIND OF PICTURED IT A DIFFERENT WAY...
HOLD IT!
DON'T EVEN FINISH THAT SENTENCE! THERE'S ONLY ONE XENA IN THIS HOUSE, AND THAT'S...
DUMB DOOR JAMMED...
WHOA!
WAK!
UH OH... THAT DIDN'T HIT YOU, DID IT?
KATCHOO?
ARE YOU OKAY?
TWEET
TWEET?

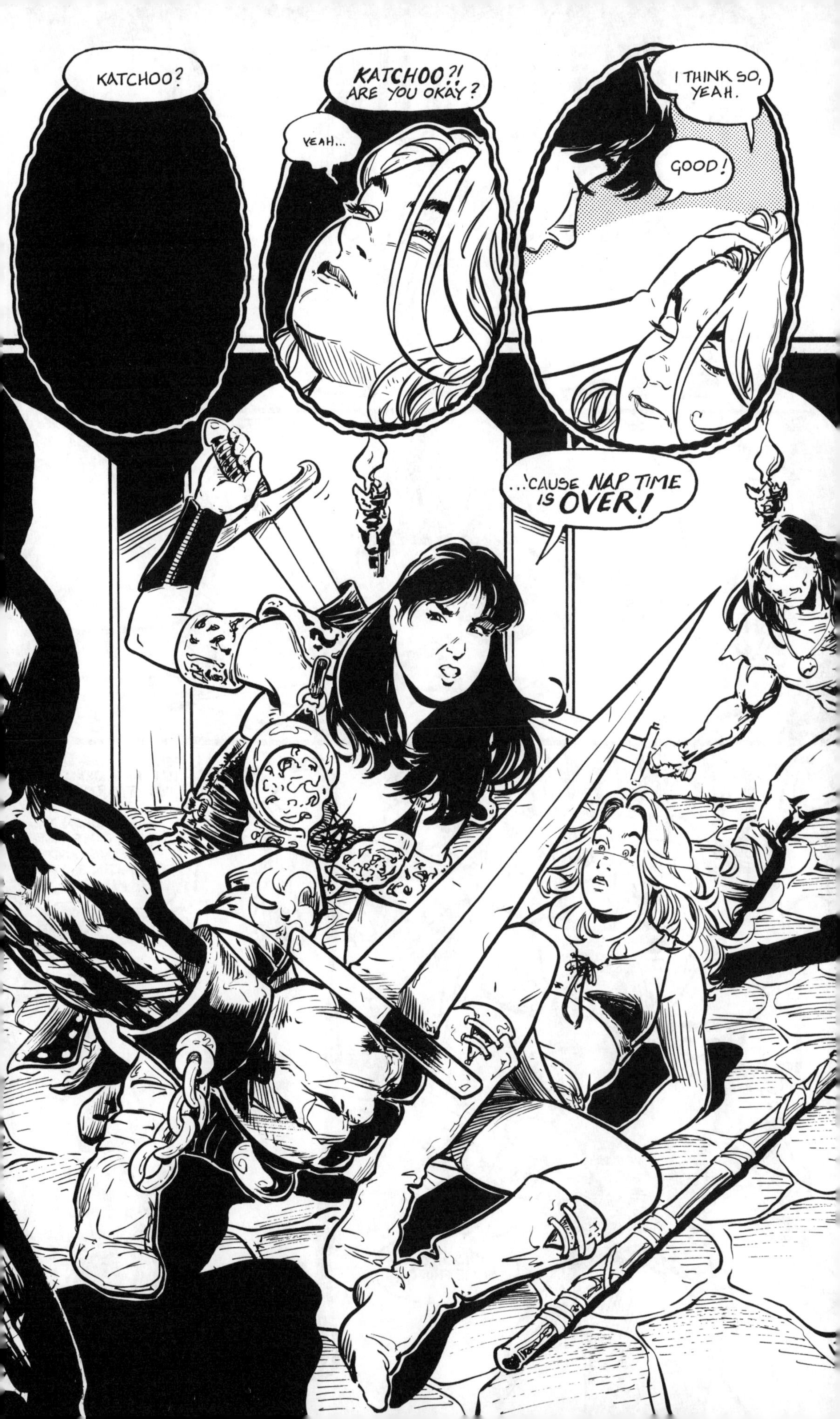
KATCHOO?
KATCHOO?! ARE YOU OKAY?
YEAH...
I THINK SO, YEAH.
GOOD!
...'CAUSE NAP TIME IS OVER!

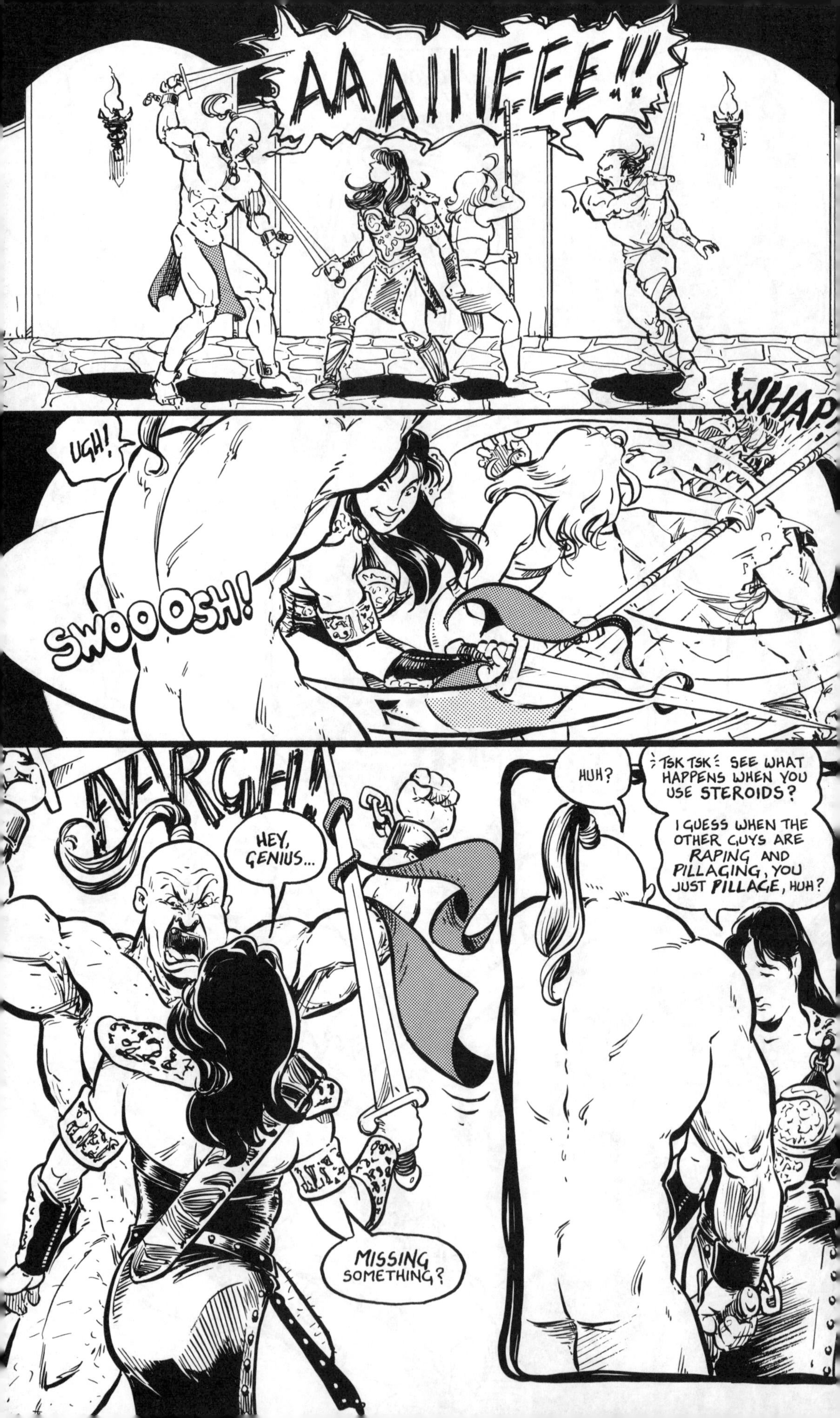
AAAIIEEE!!
WHAP!
UGH!
SWOOOSH!
ARRGH!
HEY, GENIUS...
MISSING SOMETHING?
HUH?
TSK TSK SEE WHAT HAPPENS WHEN YOU USE STEROIDS?
I GUESS WHEN THE OTHER GUYS ARE RAPING AND PILLAGING, YOU JUST PILLAGE, HUH?

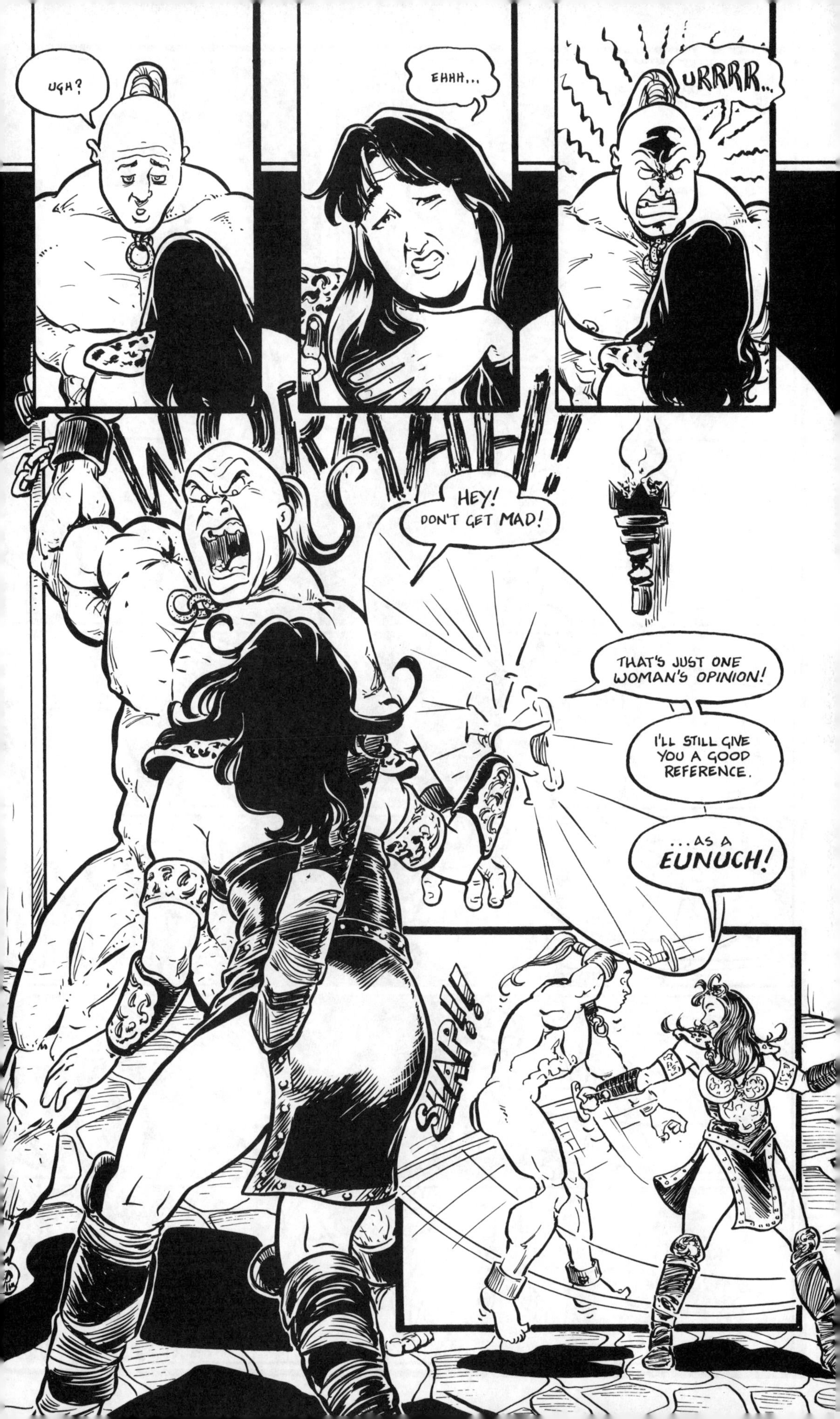
UGH?
EHHH...
URRRR...
WHOAAAHH!!
HEY!
DON'T GET MAD!
THAT'S JUST ONE
WOMAN'S OPINION!
I'LL STILL GIVE
YOU A GOOD
REFERENCE.
...AS A
EUNUCH!
SNAP!!!

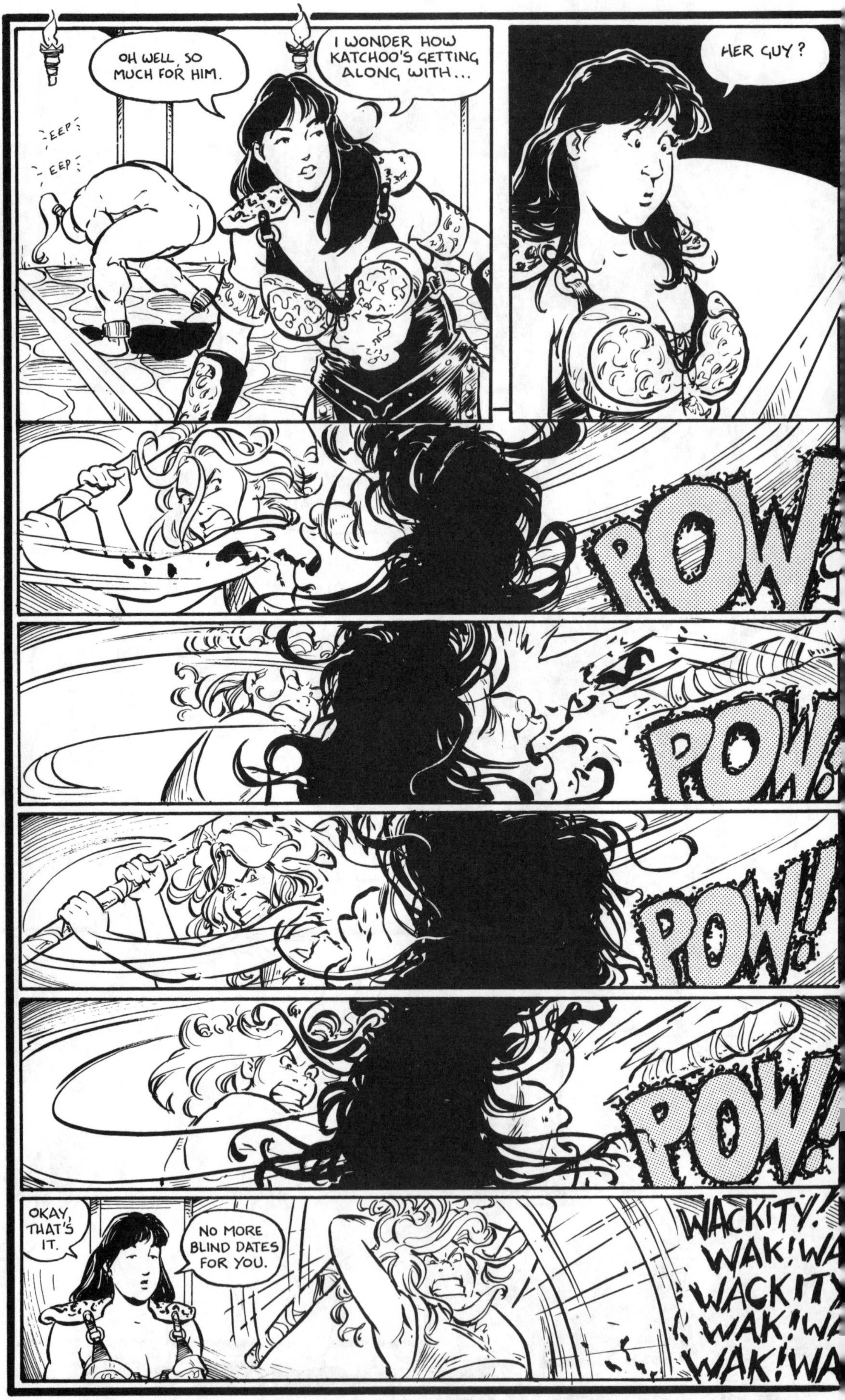
OH WELL, SO MUCH FOR HIM.
I WONDER HOW KATCHOO'S GETTING ALONG WITH...
EEP
EEP
HER GUY?
POW
POW
POW!
POW
OKAY, THAT'S IT.
NO MORE BLIND DATES FOR YOU.
WACKITY! WAK! WA WACKITY WAK! WA WAK! WA

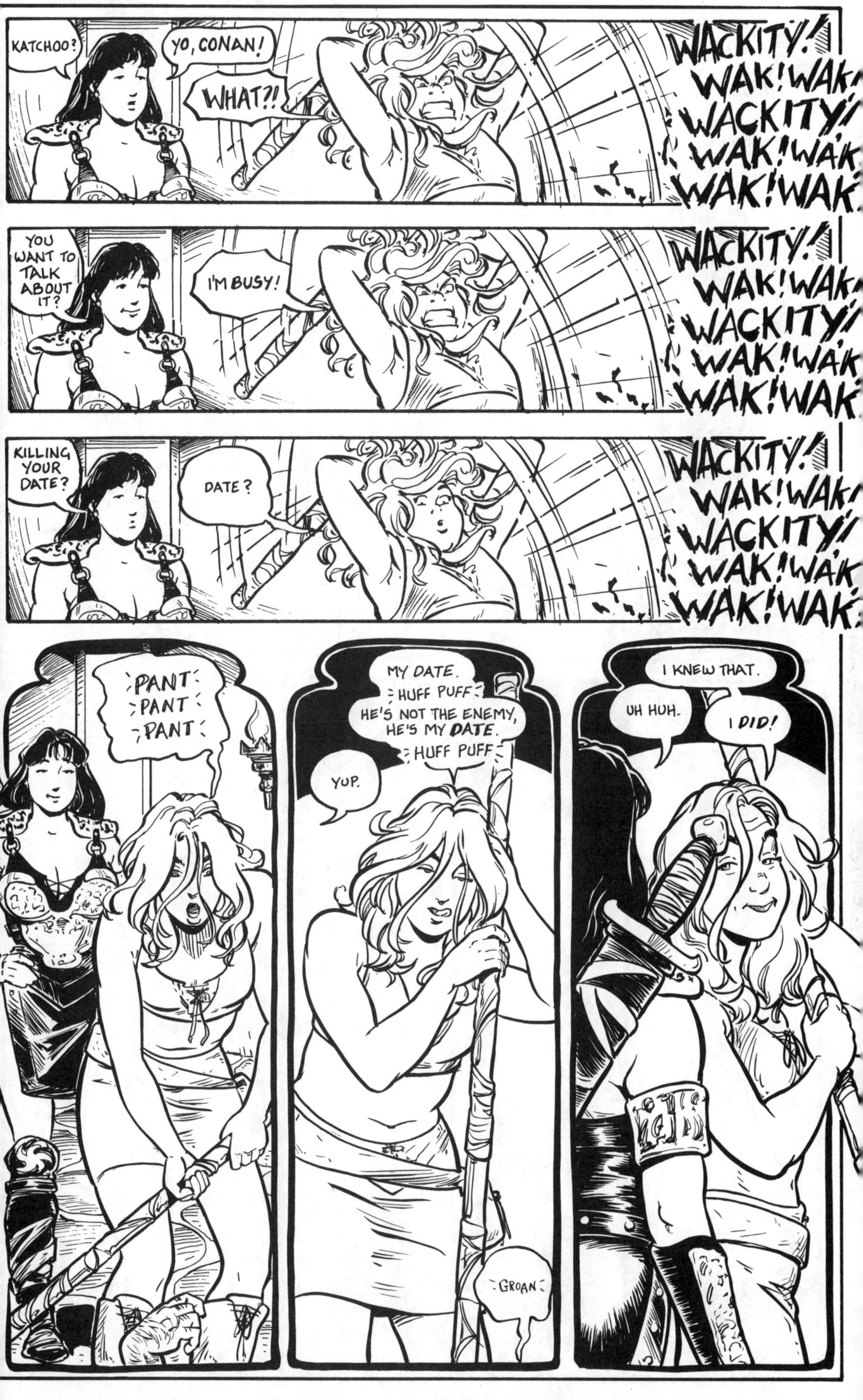
KATCHOO?
YO, CONAN!
WHAT?!
WACKITY! WAK! WAK! WACKITY! WAK! WAK! WAK! WAK
YOU WANT TO TALK ABOUT IT?
I'M BUSY!
WACKITY! WAK! WAK! WACKITY! WAK! WAK! WAK! WAK
KILLING YOUR DATE?
DATE?
WACKITY! WAK! WAK! WACKITY! WAK! WAK! WAK! WAK
PANT PANT PANT
MY DATE.
HUFF PUFF
HE'S NOT THE ENEMY, HE'S MY DATE.
HUFF PUFF
YUP.
GROAN
I KNEW THAT.
UH HUH.
I DID!

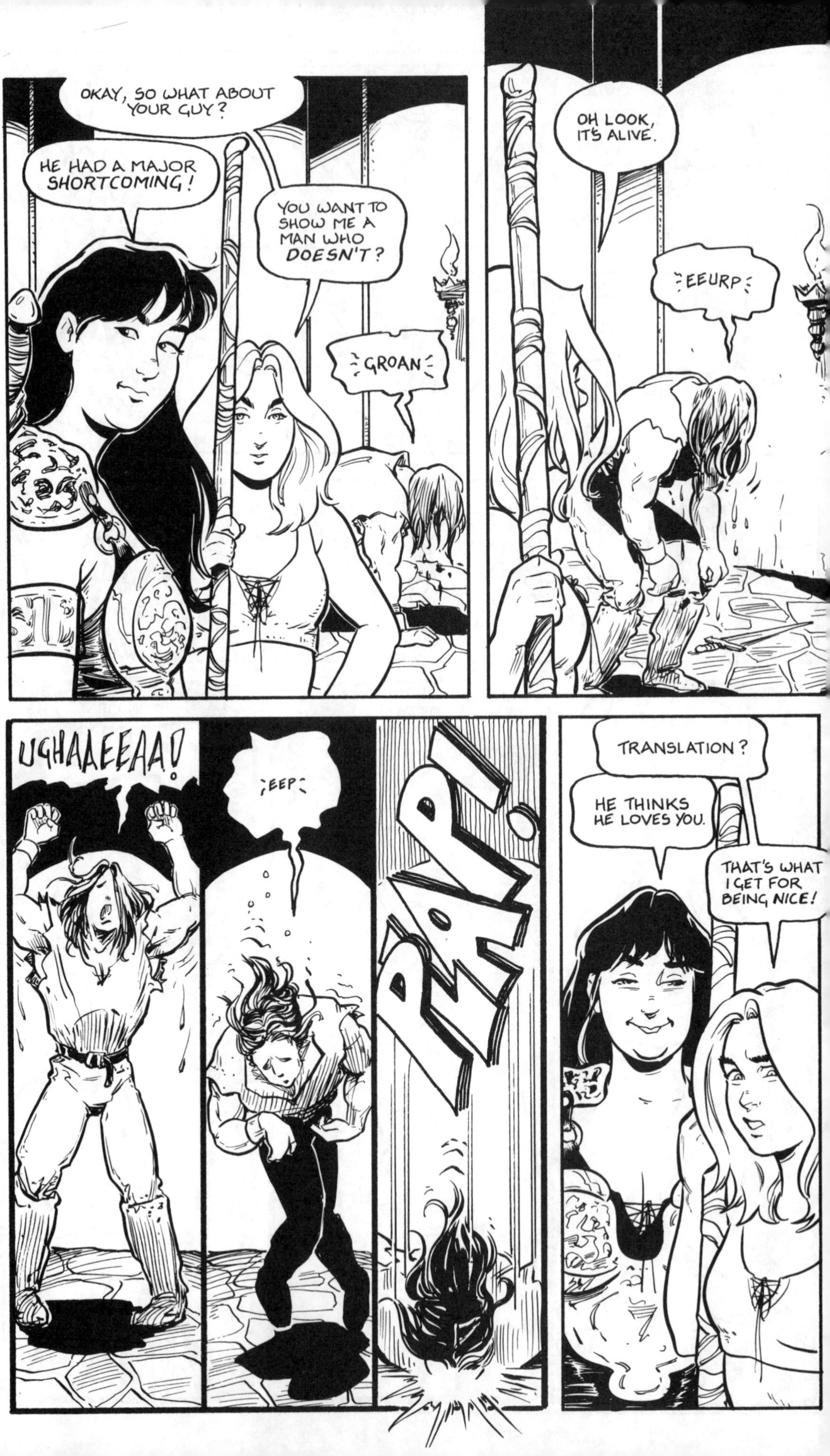
OKAY, SO WHAT ABOUT YOUR GUY?
HE HAD A MAJOR SHORTCOMING!
YOU WANT TO SHOW ME A MAN WHO DOESN'T?
GROAN
OH LOOK, IT'S ALIVE.
EEURP
UGHAAEEAA!
EEP
PAM!
TRANSLATION?
HE THINKS HE LOVES YOU.
THAT'S WHAT I GET FOR BEING NICE!

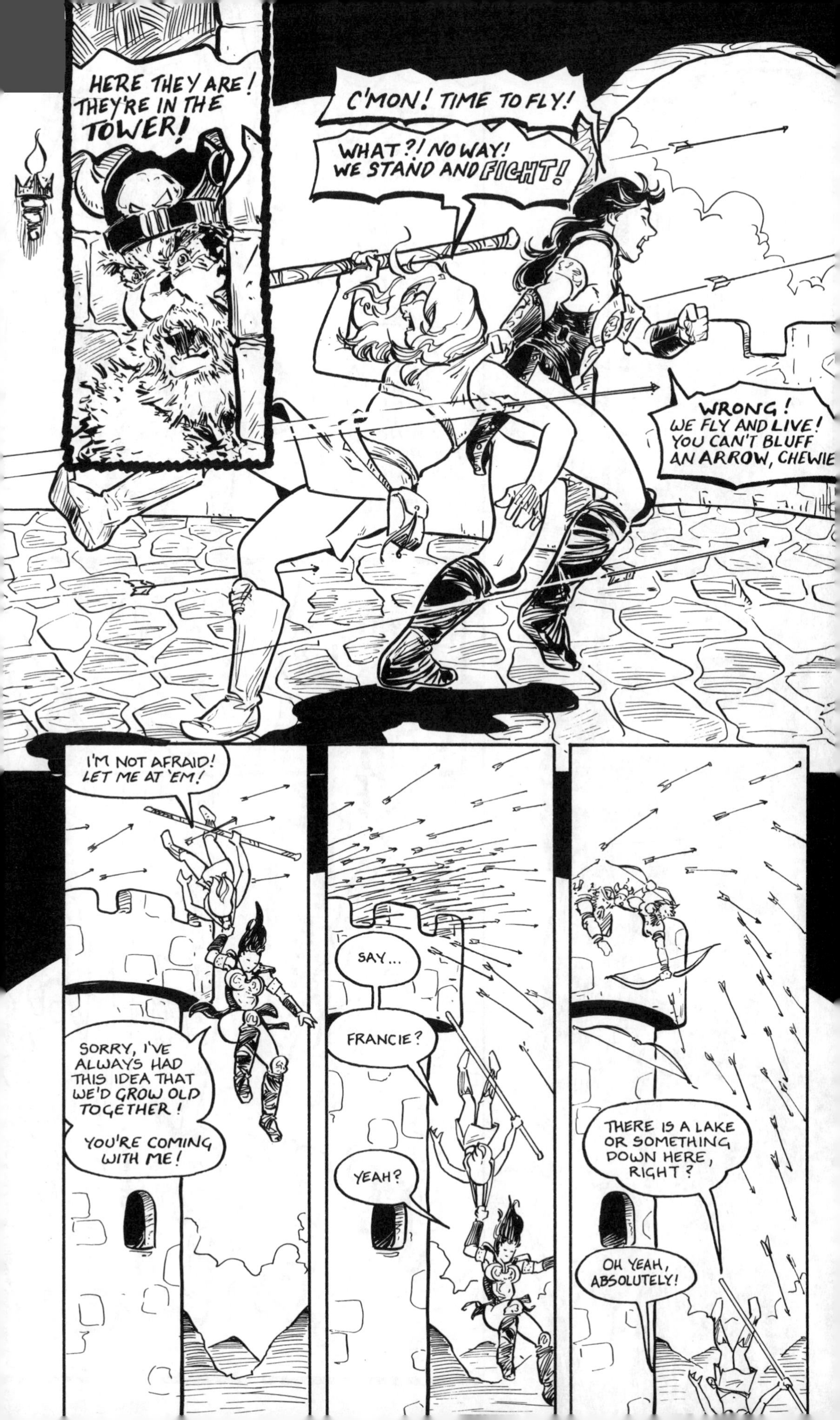
HERE THEY ARE! THEY'RE IN THE TOWER!
C'MON! TIME TO FLY!
WHAT?! NO WAY! WE STAND AND FIGHT!
WRONG! WE FLY AND LIVE! YOU CAN'T BLUFF AN ARROW, CHEWIE
I'M NOT AFRAID! LET ME AT 'EM!
SORRY, I'VE ALWAYS HAD THIS IDEA THAT WE'D GROW OLD TOGETHER!
YOU'RE COMING WITH ME!
SAY...
FRANCIE?
YEAH?
THERE IS A LAKE OR SOMETHING DOWN HERE, RIGHT?
OH YEAH, ABSOLUTELY!

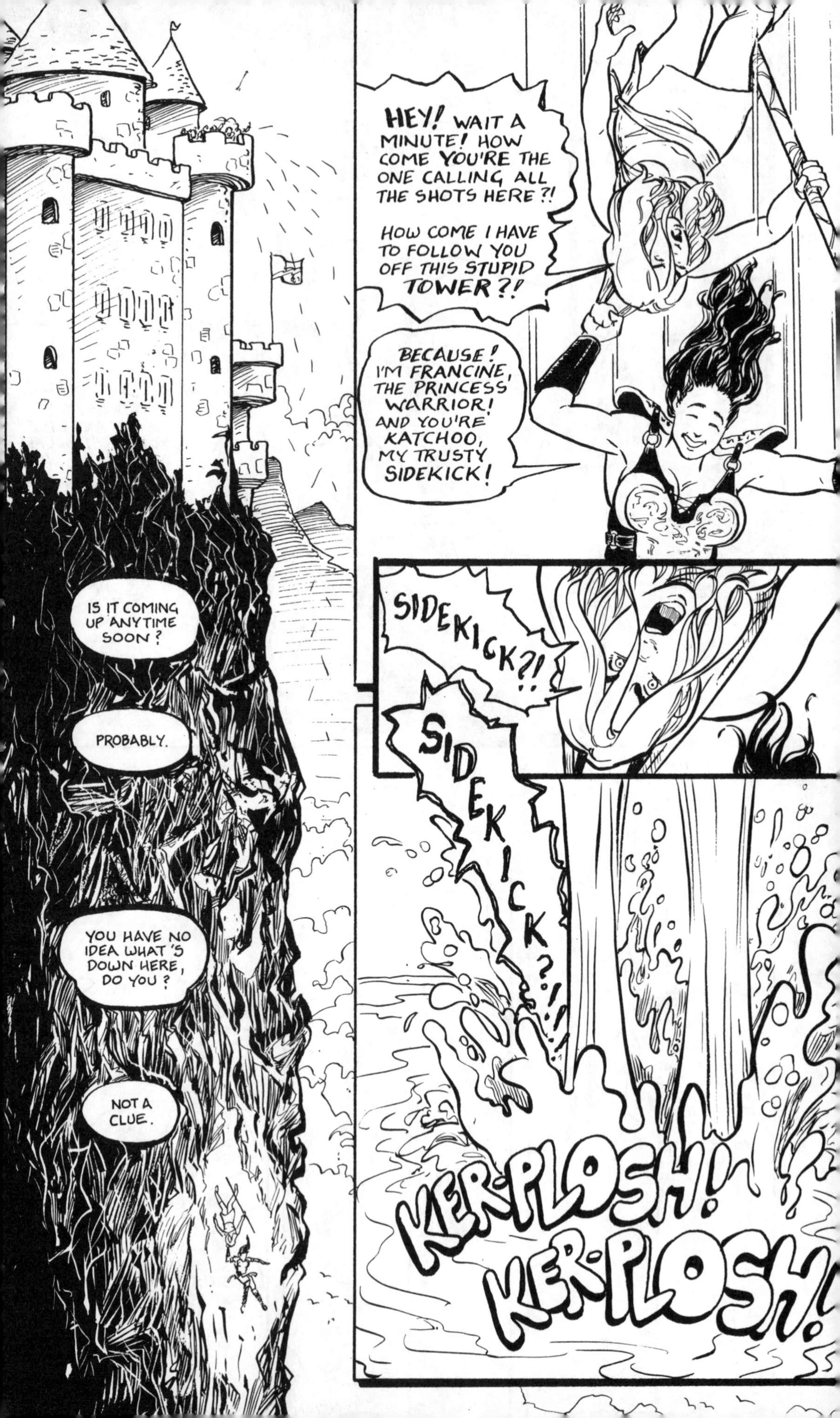
HEY! WAIT A MINUTE! HOW COME YOU'RE THE ONE CALLING ALL THE SHOTS HERE?!
HOW COME I HAVE TO FOLLOW YOU OFF THIS STUPID TOWER?!
BECAUSE! I'M FRANCINE, THE PRINCESS WARRIOR! AND YOU'RE KATCHOO, MY TRUSTY SIDEKICK!
IS IT COMING UP ANYTIME SOON?
PROBABLY.
YOU HAVE NO IDEA WHAT'S DOWN HERE, DO YOU?
NOT A CLUE.
SIDEKICK?!
SIDEKICK?!!
KER-PLOSH!
KER-PLOSH!

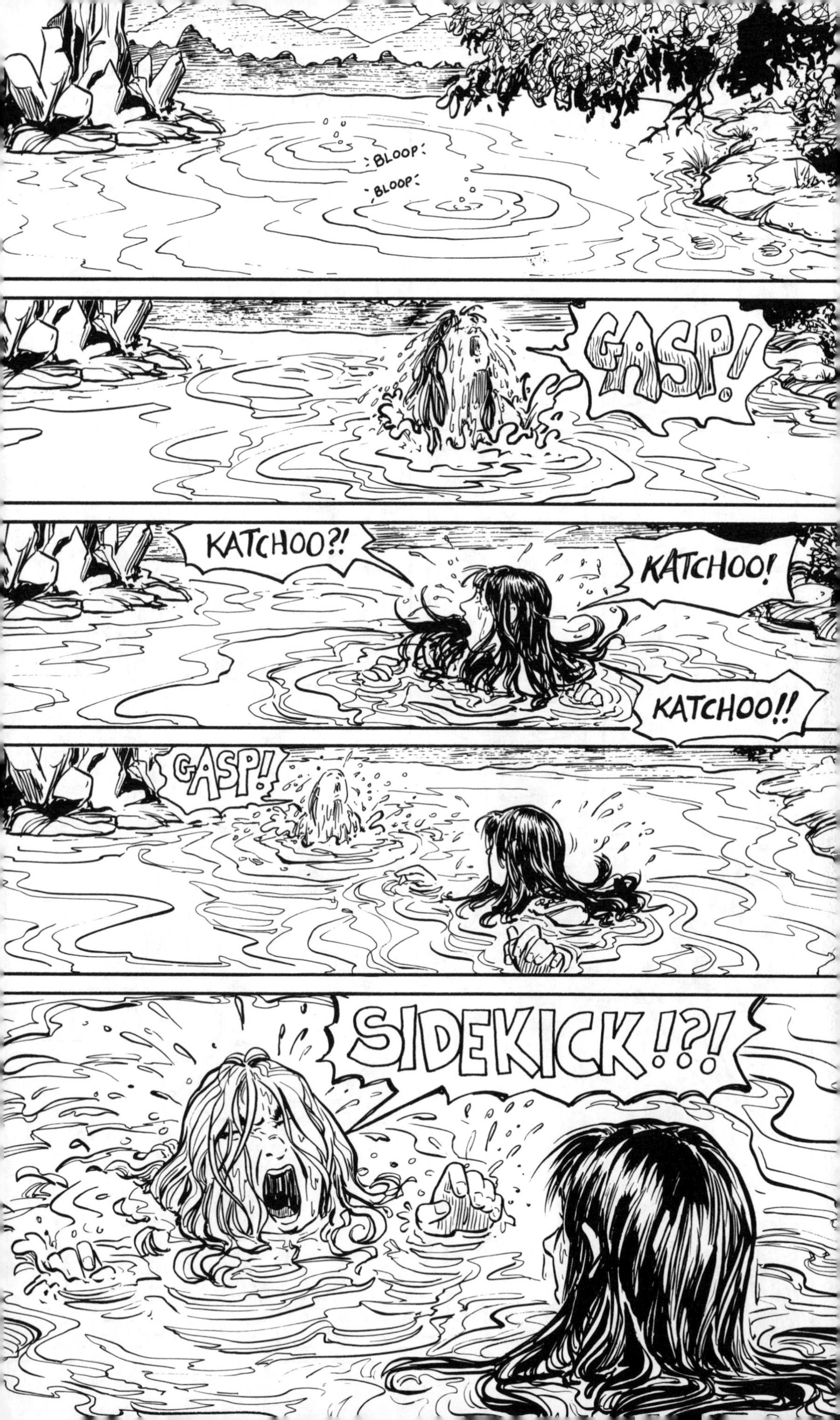
BLOOP
BLOOP
GASP!
KATCHOO?!
KATCHOO!
KATCHOO!!
GASP!
SIDEKICK!?!

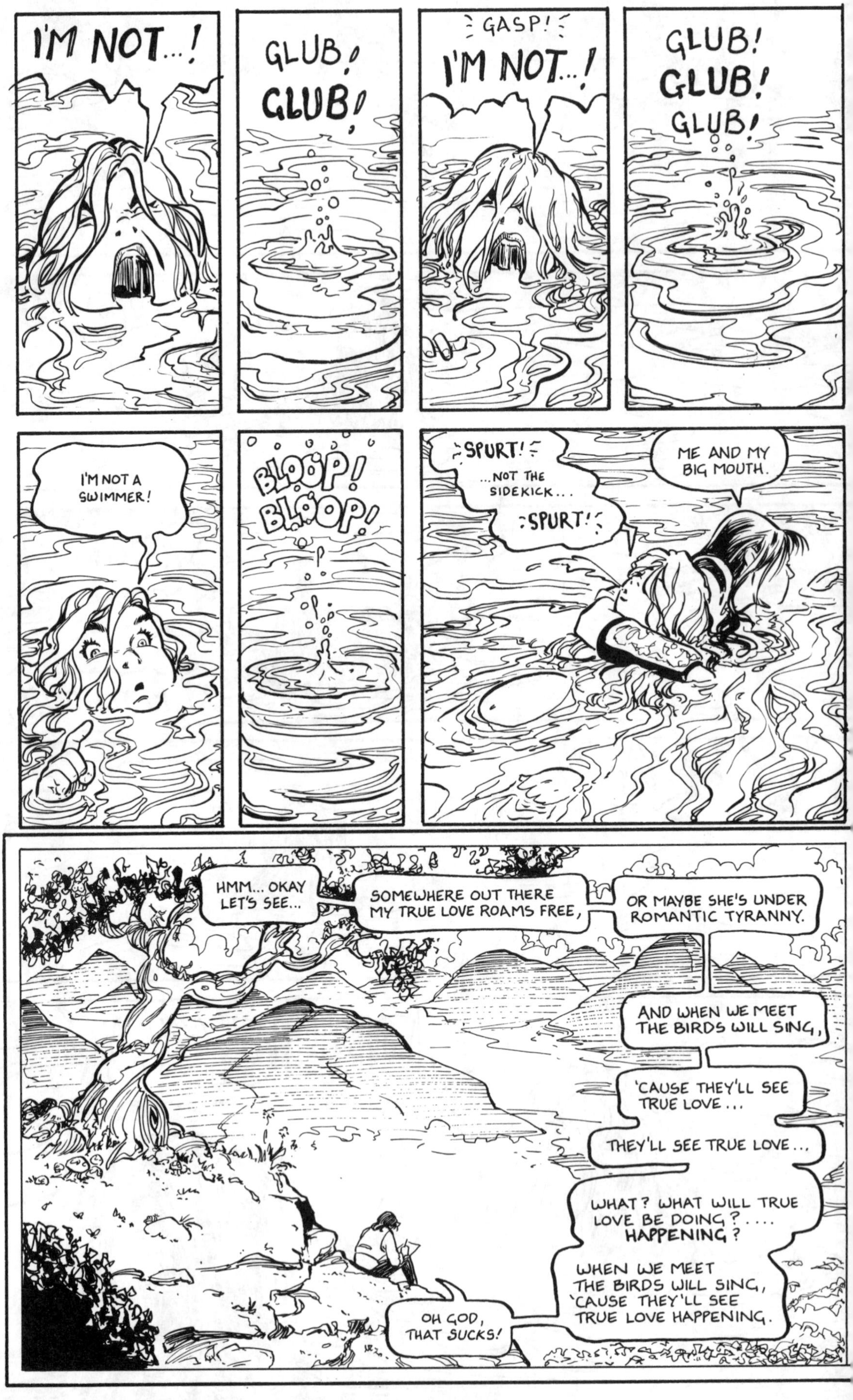

I'M NOT...!
GLUB! GLUB!
GASP!
I'M NOT...!
GLUB! GLUB! GLUB!
I'M NOT A SWIMMER!
BLOOP! BLOOP!
SPURT! ...NOT THE SIDEKICK... SPURT!
ME AND MY BIG MOUTH.
HMM... OKAY LET'S SEE...
SOMEWHERE OUT THERE MY TRUE LOVE ROAMS FREE,
OR MAYBE SHE'S UNDER ROMANTIC TYRANNY.
AND WHEN WE MEET THE BIRDS WILL SING,
'CAUSE THEY'LL SEE TRUE LOVE...
THEY'LL SEE TRUE LOVE...,
WHAT? WHAT WILL TRUE LOVE BE DOING?.... HAPPENING?
WHEN WE MEET THE BIRDS WILL SING, 'CAUSE THEY'LL SEE TRUE LOVE HAPPENING.
OH GOD, THAT SUCKS!

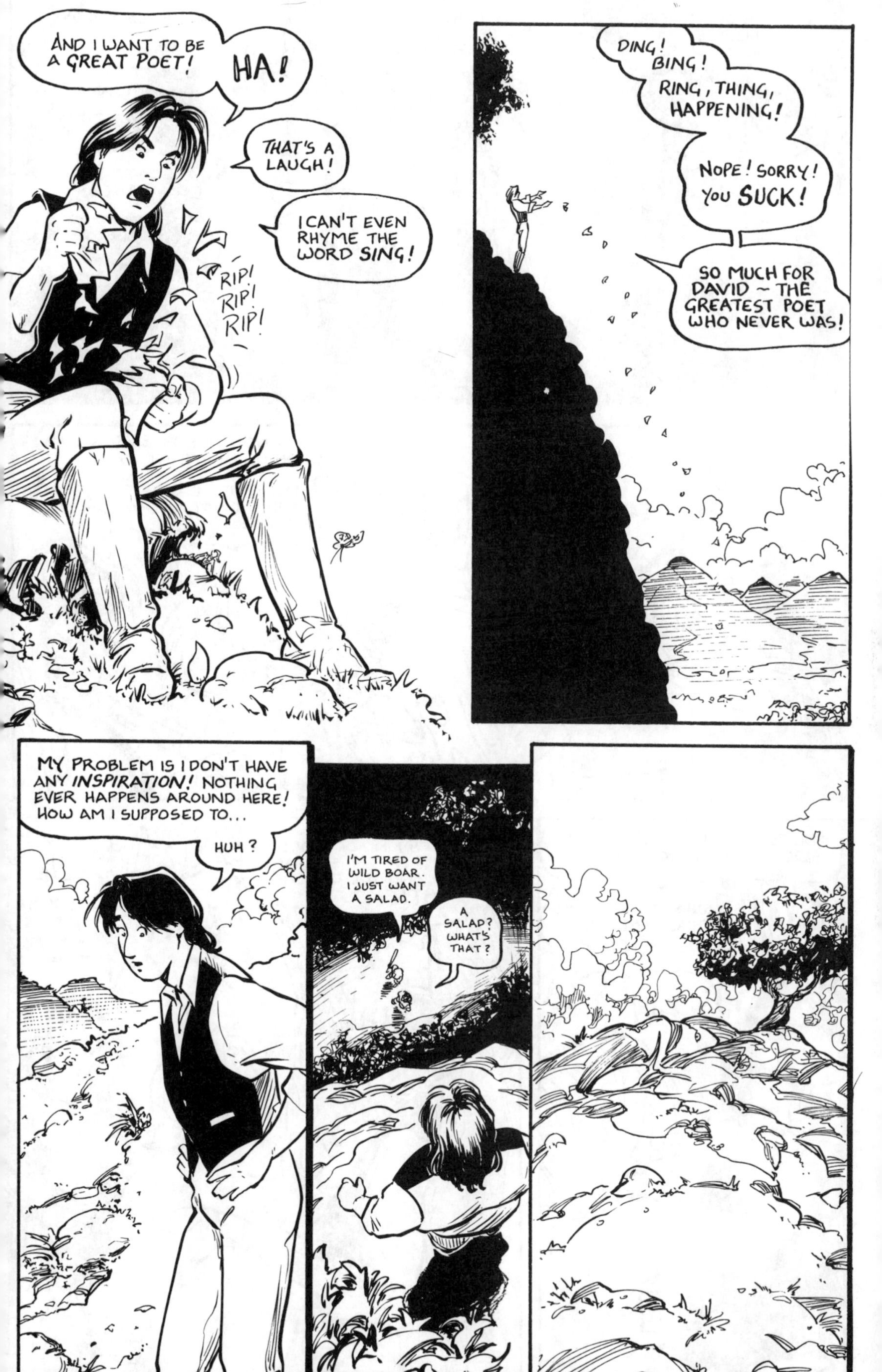
AND I WANT TO BE A GREAT POET!
HA!
THAT'S A LAUGH!
I CAN'T EVEN RHYME THE WORD SING!
RIP! RIP! RIP!
DING! BING! RING, THING, HAPPENING!
NOPE! SORRY! YOU SUCK!
SO MUCH FOR DAVID ~ THE GREATEST POET WHO NEVER WAS!
MY PROBLEM IS I DON'T HAVE ANY INSPIRATION! NOTHING EVER HAPPENS AROUND HERE! HOW AM I SUPPOSED TO...
HUH?
I'M TIRED OF WILD BOAR. I JUST WANT A SALAD.
A SALAD? WHAT'S THAT?

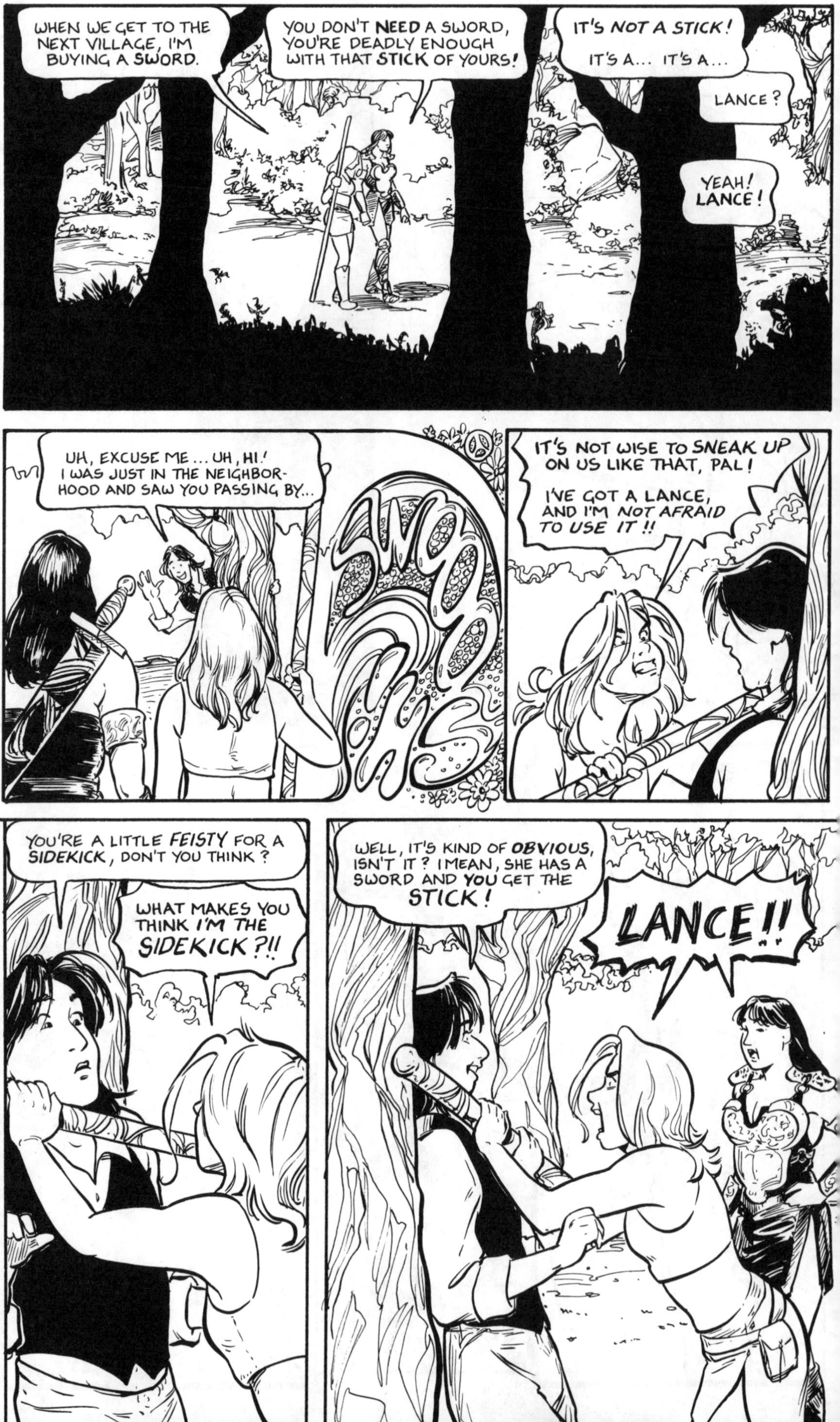
WHEN WE GET TO THE NEXT VILLAGE, I'M BUYING A SWORD.
YOU DON'T NEED A SWORD, YOU'RE DEADLY ENOUGH WITH THAT STICK OF YOURS!
IT'S NOT A STICK! IT'S A... IT'S A...
LANCE?
YEAH! LANCE!
UH, EXCUSE ME... UH, HI! I WAS JUST IN THE NEIGHBORHOOD AND SAW YOU PASSING BY...
IT'S NOT WISE TO SNEAK UP ON US LIKE THAT, PAL!
I'VE GOT A LANCE, AND I'M NOT AFRAID TO USE IT!!
YOU'RE A LITTLE FEISTY FOR A SIDEKICK, DON'T YOU THINK?
WHAT MAKES YOU THINK I'M THE SIDEKICK?!!
WELL, IT'S KIND OF OBVIOUS, ISN'T IT? I MEAN, SHE HAS A SWORD AND YOU GET THE STICK!
LANCE!!

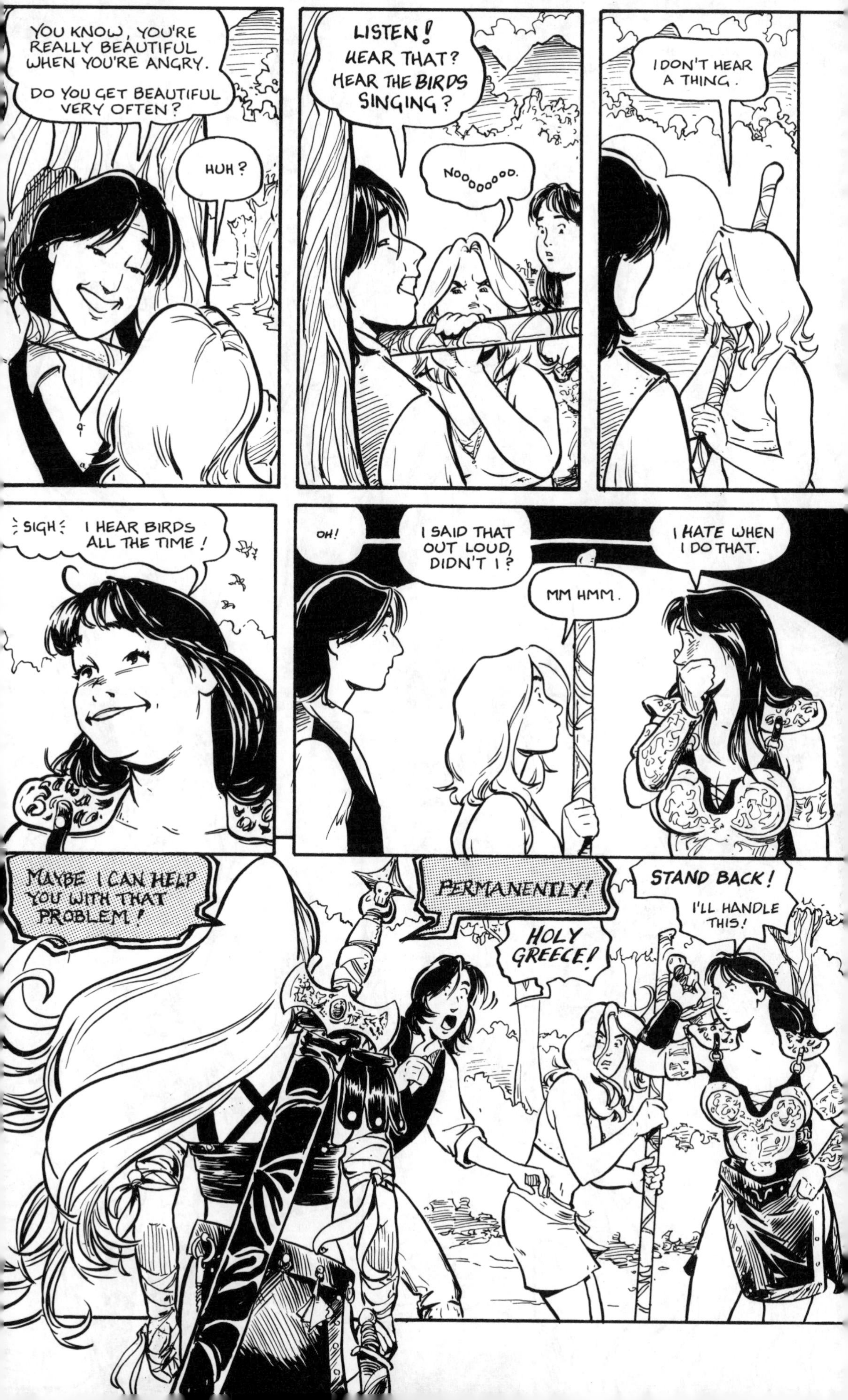
YOU KNOW, YOU'RE REALLY BEAUTIFUL WHEN YOU'RE ANGRY.
DO YOU GET BEAUTIFUL VERY OFTEN?
HUH?
LISTEN! HEAR THAT? HEAR THE BIRDS SINGING?
NOOOOOOOO.
I DON'T HEAR A THING.
SIGH I HEAR BIRDS ALL THE TIME!
OH!
I SAID THAT OUT LOUD, DIDN'T I?
MM HMM.
I HATE WHEN I DO THAT.
MAYBE I CAN HELP YOU WITH THAT PROBLEM!
PERMANENTLY!
HOLY GREECE!
STAND BACK!
I'LL HANDLE THIS!

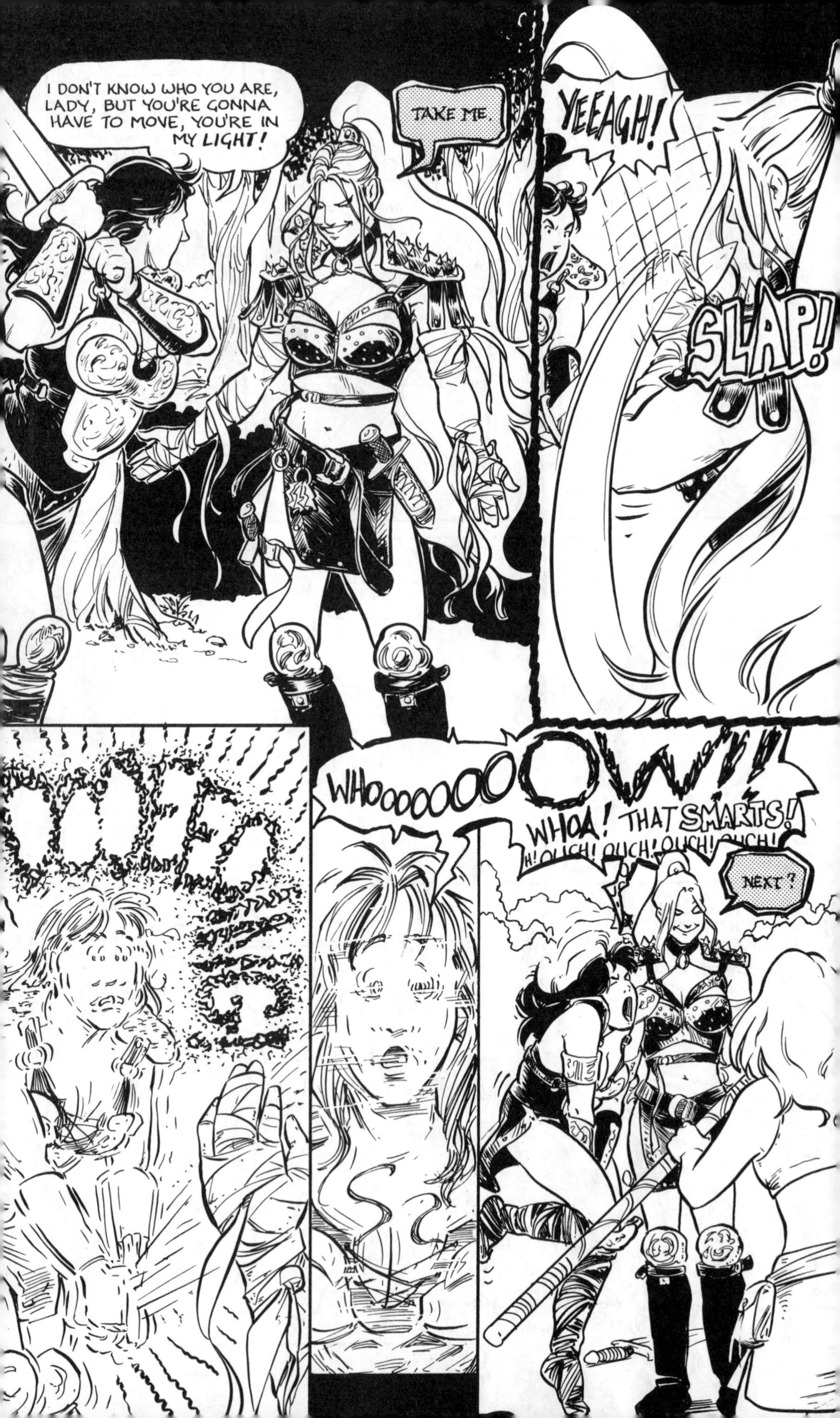
I DON'T KNOW WHO YOU ARE, LADY, BUT YOU'RE GONNA HAVE TO MOVE, YOU'RE IN MY LIGHT!
TAKE ME.
YEEAGH!
SLAP!
OOF
WHOOOOOOOOOOW!!
WHOA! THAT SMARTS!
H! OUCH! OUCH! OUCH! OUCH!
NEXT?

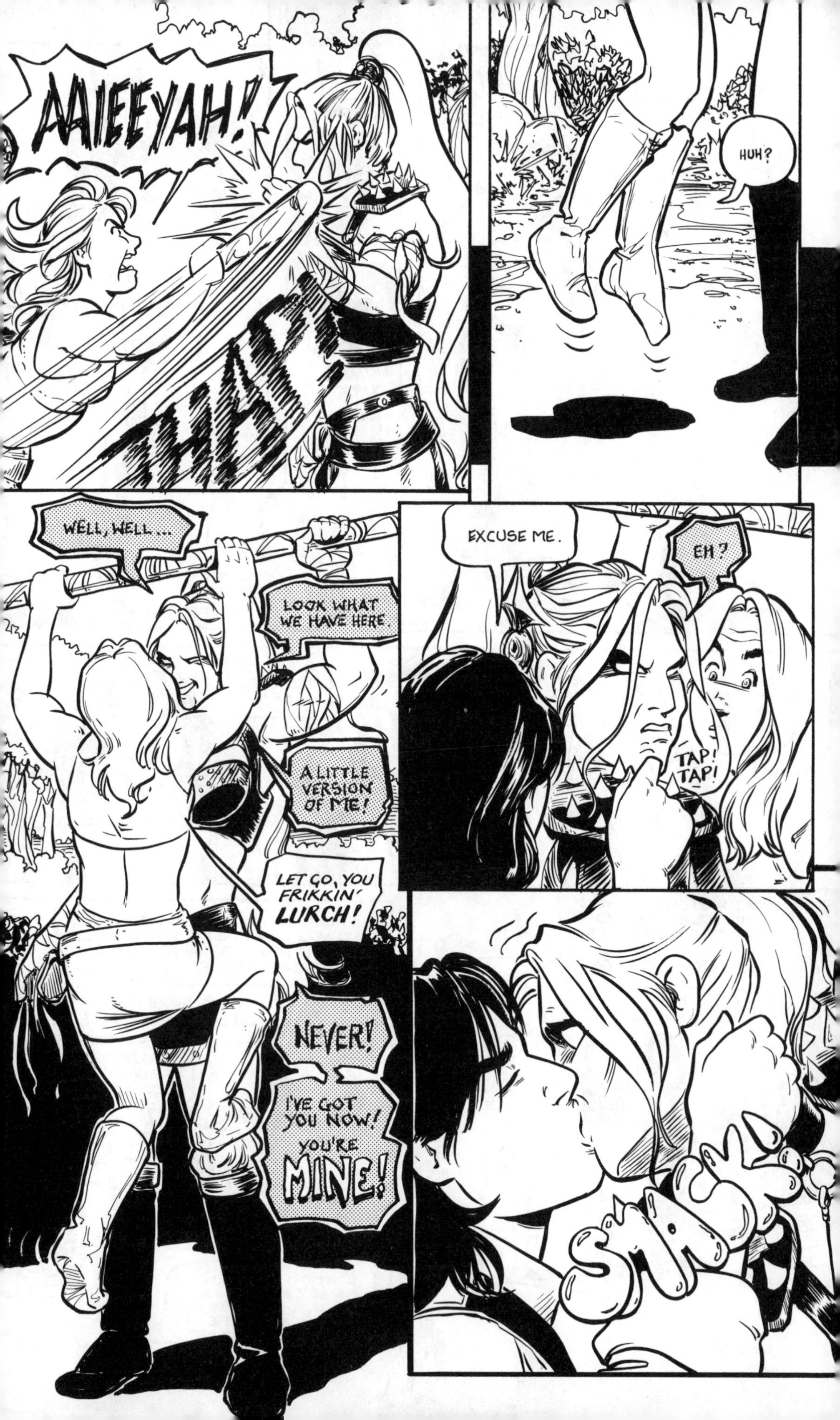
AAIEEYAH!
THWAP!
HUH?
WELL, WELL...
LOOK WHAT WE HAVE HERE.
A LITTLE VERSION OF ME!
LET GO, YOU FRIKKIN' LURCH!
NEVER!
I'VE GOT YOU NOW! YOU'RE MINE!
EXCUSE ME.
EH?
TAP! TAP!

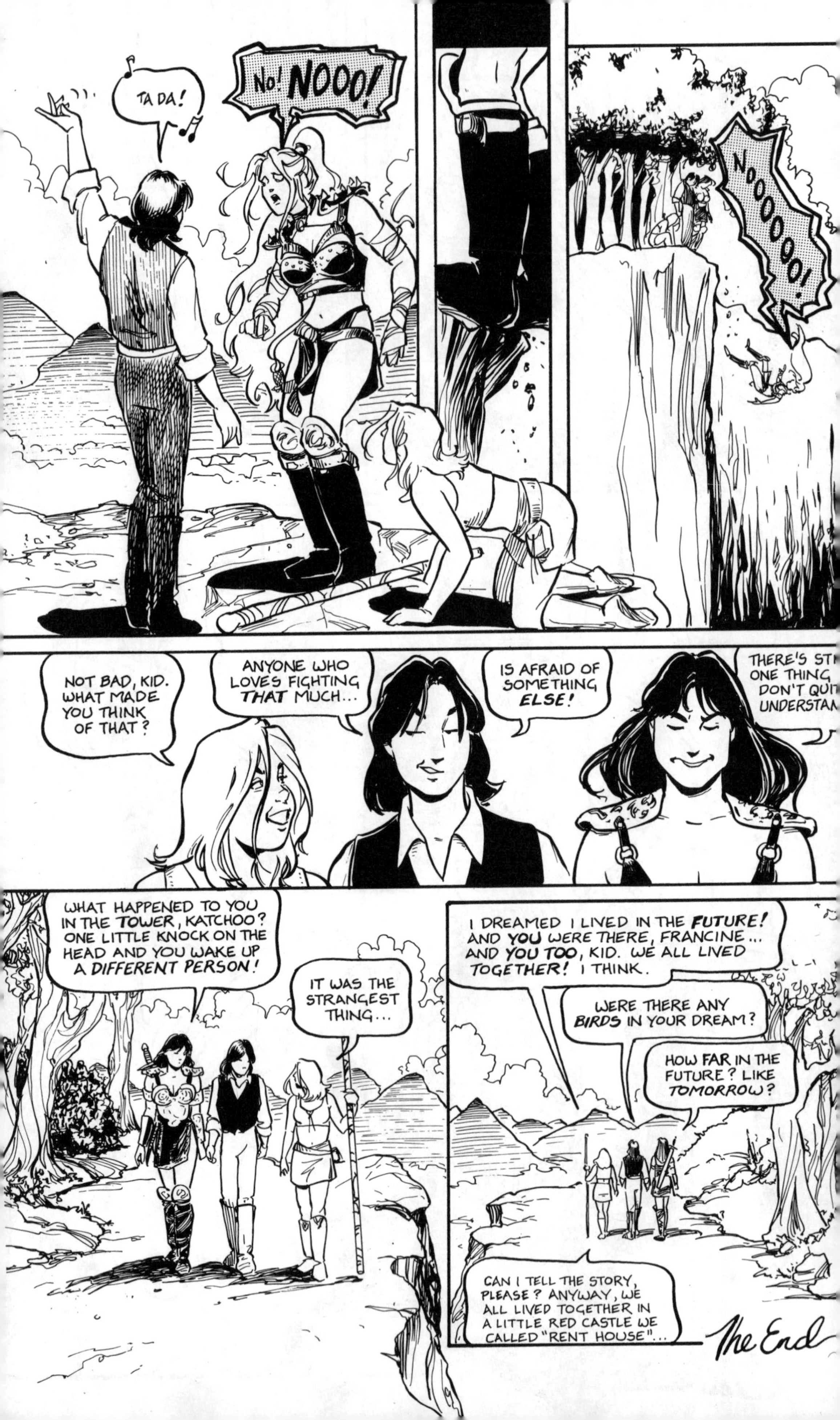
TA DA!
No! NOOO!
NOOOOOO!
NOT BAD, KID. WHAT MADE YOU THINK OF THAT?
ANYONE WHO LOVES FIGHTING THAT MUCH...
IS AFRAID OF SOMETHING ELSE!
THERE'S STI
ONE THING
DON'T QUI
UNDERSTAN
WHAT HAPPENED TO YOU IN THE TOWER, KATCHOO? ONE LITTLE KNOCK ON THE HEAD AND YOU WAKE UP A DIFFERENT PERSON!
IT WAS THE STRANGEST THING...
I DREAMED I LIVED IN THE FUTURE! AND YOU WERE THERE, FRANCINE... AND YOU TOO, KID. WE ALL LIVED TOGETHER! I THINK.
WERE THERE ANY BIRDS IN YOUR DREAM?
HOW FAR IN THE FUTURE? LIKE TOMORROW?
CAN I TELL THE STORY, PLEASE? ANYWAY, WE ALL LIVED TOGETHER IN A LITTLE RED CASTLE WE CALLED "RENT HOUSE"...
The End